Wisdom 21:
Shaping the Culture of Peace in a Multilateral World

A Compilation of Articles
by Intergovernmental Organizations

Compiled by The Goi Peace Foundation
Patrick Uwe Petit (Ed.)

D1718204

Goi Peace
Foundation

United Nations
60
A Time for Renewal

Publisher:

The Goi Peace Foundation

Heiwa Daiichi Building

1–4–5 Hirakawacho

Chiyoda-ku, Tokyo 102-0093; Japan

http://www.goipeace.or.jp

Editor:

Patrick Uwe Petit (E-mail: goipeace@web.de)

Title of Publication:

"Wisdom 21: Shaping the Culture of Peace in a Multilateral World
A Compilation of Articles by Intergovernmental Organizations"

A Publication in Honour of the Sixtieth Anniversary of the United Nations

Design and Production:

Adrian Siedentopf (E-mail: info@sidisign.de)

Printing Company: Kreiter Druck GmbH

ISBN 3-00-017490-7

* * * * * *

THE GOI PEACE FOUNDATION

GRATEFULLY ACKNOWLEDGES THE CONTRIBUTING

DISTINGUISHED INTERGOVERNMENTAL ORGANIZATIONS,

WHOSE 'VISIONS IN ACTION' ARE INVALUABLE SOURCE

OF INSPIRATION AND MOTIVATION FOR HUMANITY

AS IT SEEKS TO ACHIEVE LASTING PEACE ON EARTH

* * * * * *

In Honour of the United Nations Sixtieth Anniversary

TABLE OF CONTENTS

TABLE OF CONTENTS

INTRODUCTION

VISIONS IN ACTION

ANNEX

INTRODUCTION

INTRODUCTION

**Hiroo Saionji and Masami Saionji, President and Chairperson
The Goi Peace Foundation**

Now, as the world faces a multitude of complexly interwoven challenges and opportunities, new values and new worldviews are emerging to change the ways in which we human beings relate to each other, to our planet, and to all life on Earth. In today's globalized world, humanity is becoming inescapably aware that co-existence, cooperation, and respect for diversity are fundamental values by which all of us must live. These essential human values, which apply in all individual and societal relationships, are likewise intrinsic to the culture of peace that we wish to create: a way of living which will allow a harmonious, multifaceted, global civilization to blossom and flourish on Earth.

Each of the world's cultures is distinct and unique. Cultures always evolve over time, and they truly begin to flourish when they come into contact with others. The world's cultural diversity – its rich differences in visions, values, beliefs, practices, and forms of expression – is our common heritage and is a source of revitalization, creativity, and innovation which is as necessary to humanity as bio-diversity is to nature.

It is in this spirit of respect for cultural diversity that the Goi Peace Foundation has committed itself to building bridges of cooperation among individuals and organizations around the world, in order to stimulate a collective effort toward realizing a worldwide culture of peace.

Since its inception in 1999, the Goi Peace Foundation has been working in cooperation with the diplomatic community and with forward-looking intergovernmental organizations and institutions worldwide to conduct exchanges and joint initiatives that will promote international understanding and a prosperous future for all people on Earth. This shared vision of stimulating intercultural dialogue for the sake of peace on Earth has inspired the Goi Peace Foundation to issue a special publication on multilateralism and a culture of peace. Entitled *Wisdom 21: Shaping the Culture of Peace in a Multilateral World*, this volume calls attention to the efforts being made by various distinguished intergovernmental organizations toward creating an international culture of peace.

Central to this publication is a belief that in an increasingly interdependent world, collective decision-making for the collective good is the most effective way to move forward. In order to respect the balance among cultures and nations, decisions which have a global impact must be taken multilaterally. We believe that in the long run, no culture or nation can achieve and maintain its international objectives by acting unilaterally; nor can any single nation or cultural group claim to represent the whole of humanity, or to hold exclusive responsibility for determining humanity's future. Multilateralism, on the other hand, offers us a wide range of alternatives for dealing with global issues, because it takes all perspectives into account and allows all views to be heard. Multilateralism fosters the emergence of a mosaic of potential solutions to our collective challenges and concerns.

Out of a wish to strengthen and enhance the global trend toward increased multilateral cooperation, the Goi Peace Foundation enthusiastically supports various international programs and initiatives such as the International Decade for a Culture of Peace and Non-Violence for the Children of the World, the Global Agenda for Dialogue among Civilizations, as well as the Alliance of Civilizations Initiative, and the Promotion of Interreligious Dialogue and Cooperation for Peace.

While the United Nations is the largest forum for multilateral diplomacy and cooperation, regional and other intergovernmental organizations are playing an increasingly vital role in creating a culture of peace. Therefore, in matters of both policy and action, we believe that a closer partnership between the United Nations and regional or other intergovernmental organizations will prove to be a key ingredient in the successful resolution of the challenges facing today's world.

Wisdom 21: Shaping the Culture of Peace in a Multilateral World compiles prominent visionary articles from United Nations institutions and regional and other intergovernmental organizations, and highlights the contributions being made to the creation of a culture of peace. It aims to strengthen multilateral cooperation among intergovernmental organizations worldwide, and to facilitate the formation of a global network of multilateral mechanisms which will provide collective and holistic responses to the peace and security challenges of the 21st century.

This publication is dedicated to the 60th Anniversary of the United Nations, as well as to the 60th Anniversary of UNESCO, and it comes at a time of renewal. As Jan Eliasson, President of the 60th United Nations General Assembly, stressed in his message for UN Day, "today, we face a test of multilateralism" and "the realities of the world are a constant reminder that global action and collective efforts are now needed more than ever."

The Goi Peace Foundation would like to extend its heartfelt gratitude to the distinguished intergovernmental organizations which have contributed to this book. Their 'Visions in Action' are an invaluable source of inspiration and motivation for humanity as it seeks to achieve lasting peace on Earth. It is our hope that this publication will serve as a timely and useful resource on multilateralism, and that, as such, it will help to ensure a safer, more prosperous, peaceful future for all life on Earth.

May Peace Prevail on Earth.

The Goi Peace Foundation
Tokyo, November 2005

VISIONS IN ACTION

UNITED NATIONS
EDUCATIONAL, SCIENTIFIC AND
CULTURAL ORGANIZATION

UNITED NATIONS
EDUCATIONAL, SCIENTIFIC AND CULTURAL ORGANIZATION

Establishment

On November 16, 1945, the representatives of 37 countries met in London to sign UNESCO's Constitution which came into force on November 4, 1946 after ratification by 20 signatories.

In 1958, UNESCO's permanent Headquarters was inaugurated in Paris, France.

Today, UNESCO is comprised of 191 Member States and 6 Associate Members.

Executive Head

H. E. Mr. Koïchiro Matsuura, Director-General of UNESCO

Objectives

UNESCO's ambitious goal is to build peace in the minds of men through education, the sciences, culture, communication and information.

It promotes international co-operation among its Member States and Associate Members in the fields as mentioned obove.

UNESCO works to create the conditions for true dialogue, based upon respect for commonly shared values and the dignity of each civilization and culture.

Today, UNESCO works as a laboratory of ideas and a standard-setter to forge universal agreements on emerging ethical issues.

This specialized UN agency also serves as a clearinghouse – that disseminates and shares information and knowledge – while helping Member States to build their human and institutional capacities in diverse fields.

Following a proposal by UNESCO, the United Nations General Assembly in 1998 (resolution A/52/13) defined the Culture of Peace as consisting of values, attitudes and behaviours that reject violence and endeavour to prevent conflicts by addressing their root causes with a view to solving problems through dialogue and negotiation among individuals, groups and nations. The 1999 United Nations Declaration and Programme of Action on a Culture of Peace (resolution A/53/243) called for everyone – governments, civil society, the media, parents, teachers, politicians, scientists, artists, NGOs and the entire United Nations system – to assume responsibility in this respect. It staked out eight action areas for actors at national, regional and international levels:

1. Fostering a culture of peace through education;
2. Promoting sustainable economic and social development;
3. Promoting respect for all human rights;
4. Ensuring equality between women and men;
5. Fostering democratic participation;
6. Advancing understanding, tolerance and solidarity;
7. Supporting participatory communication
    and the free flow of information and knowledge;
8. Promoting international peace and security.

Contact Information

UNESCO

7, Place de Fontenoy
75352 Paris 07 SP
France

Telephone: + 33 (0) 1 45 68 10 00
Fax: + 33 (0) 1 45 67 16 90

Internet: **http://www.unesco.org**

United Nations Educational, Scientific and Cultural Organization

United Nations
Educational, Scientific and Cultural Organization

H. E. Mr. Koïchiro Matsuura, Director-General of UNESCO

Sixty years ago, UNESCO Member States committed themselves to a noble challenge. They stated in the preamble to the UNESCO Constitution that "Since wars begin in the minds of men, it is in the minds of men that the defences of peace must be constructed," and entrusted the Organization to pursue this mission through international cooperation in the areas of education, culture, the sciences and communication and information.

Today, this mission is more relevant than ever. We are witnessing a rapidly changing world marked by powerful, interrelated and sometimes opposing forces: a reinforced globalization fueling economic growth and prosperity in some parts of the world, while leaving others behind; persistent inequalities and poverty between and within regions, states and communities; an intensification of economic, cultural and political exchanges fuelled by the communications revolution; a degradation of the world's natural environment and an intensification of natural disasters; the re-emergence of ethnic, political and cultural violence, conflicts and various forms of terrorism and organized crime in many parts of the world; and rapid political, social, demographic and cultural transformations within states and on the regional and global levels.

The United Nations has responded to this complex set of challenges by intensifying its work in all fields of international cooperation. Special focus has been put on the three interrelated areas of development, security and human rights, as set out in the Secretary-General's report "In Larger Freedom" and as captured in the United Nations Millennium Declaration adopted in September 2000. Likewise, the United Nations General Assembly had declared the period of 2001 to 2010 the International Decade for a Culture of Peace and Non-Violence for the Children of the World and designated UNESCO as the lead agency within the United Nations system for this Decade. UNESCO was thereby entrusted with the task of coordinating and developing a culture of peace in cooperation with governments, other United Nations agencies and programmes, and civil society. The General Assembly defined the culture of peace as a "set of values, attitudes, traditions and modes of behaviour and ways of life that reject violence and prevent conflicts by tackling their root causes to solve problems through dialogue and negotiation among individuals, groups and nations"[1] and set eight main areas for intervention in its Declaration and Programme of Action:

1. Fostering a culture of peace through education;

2. Promoting sustainable economic and social development;

3. Promoting respect for all human rights;

4. Ensuring equality between women and men;

5. Fostering democratic participation;

6. Advancing understanding, tolerance and solidarity;

7. Supporting participatory communication and
   the free flow of information and knowledge;

8. Promoting international peace and security.

This ambitious Programme of Action resulted from an evolution of the concept of peace, which is understood not only as the absence of international armed conflict but also as "intranational" peace and the safety of individuals worldwide. What is today known as "human security", both as a notion and a concerted effort by several United Nations agencies, contributes to the establishment of a culture of peace, notably through its multidimensional and holistic approach, reshaping the notion of security that traditionally is a prerogative of the state. Both the concept of a culture of peace and the idea of human security put the accent on the people – individuals – instead of nations, stressing that peace and security can only be achieved if they are based on human development rather than on a narrowly-conceived view of security. As stated in the report of the High-level Panel on Threats, Challenges and Change, A More Secure World, Our Shared Responsibility: "Any event or process that leads to large-scale death or lessening of life chances … is a threat to international security". This, of course, requires the effective participation of civil society in the search for peace. The programme of action of the Decade, therefore, stresses that United Nations agencies and programmes cannot act alone, they must involve civil society, professional associations and networks, specialized NGOs, universities and research

United Nations Educational, Scientific and Cultural Organization

institutes which share their concerns and values and whose involvement in education, training and monitoring is vital to the cause of peace.

At UNESCO, the Programme of Action on a culture of peace is implemented by drawing on all of the domains of competence of the Organization. In fact, UNESCO chose as its unifying theme for the period 2002–2007 "to contribute to peace and human development in an era of globalization through education, the sciences, culture and communication". Such an approach explains UNESCO's focus on two cross-cutting themes in all of its programmes: 1) the eradication of poverty, especially extreme poverty; and 2) the contribution of information and communication technologies to the development of education, science and culture and the construction of a knowledge society.

UNESCO hopes thereby to make a concrete contribution to the reduction of the manifold divisions around the world: the divisions between the informed and the uninformed, the rich and the poor, the secure and the endangered, men and women. Such an approach is more urgent than ever, as poverty continues to be one of the most fundamental divides afflicting the world. More than a billion people in the world live on less than a dollar per day; just over two percent of women die in childbirth in the developing world; 11 million children die before the age of five every year from preventable or curable diseases. The injustices, exclusions, deprivations and inequalities engendered by poverty, and especially extreme poverty, must be dealt with effectively, as must their root causes, if social justice and cohesion, economic and social progress, democracy and ultimately peace are to be strengthened.

UNESCO's medium-term vision can only be achieved through sustained action in all of its fields of competence. For 2006 and 2007, priority is given to programmes on basic education for all, water and associated ecosystems, the ethics of science and technology (especially bioethics), the promotion of cultural diversity (with particular emphasis on tangible and intangible cultural heritage) and empowering people through access to information and knowledge (with special emphasis on freedom of expression).

Quality Education for All

One of the most powerful tools in the struggle against ignorance and violence is quality education. The right to education, as a fundamental human right, is at the very heart of UNESCO's mission and is an integral part of its constitutional mandate. As an empowering right, education is the primary vehicle by which economically and socially marginalized children and adults can lift themselves out of poverty, and obtain the means to participate fully in their communities. The commitment to work for a world where every person is educated was captured internationally in the Dakar Framework for Action of 2000, which formulated six Education for All (EFA) goals. It assigned to the international community the tasks of reaching the following goals by 2015:

i) expanding and improving comprehensive early childhood care and education, especially for the most vulnerable and disadvantaged children;

ii) ensuring that by 2015 all children, particularly girls, children in difficult circumstances and those belonging to ethnic minorities, have access to and complete free and compulsory primary education of good quality;

iii) ensuring that the learning needs of all young people and adults are met through equitable access to appropriate learning and life skills programmes;

iv) achieving a 50 per cent improvement in levels of adult literacy by 2015, especially for women, and equitable access to basic and continuing education for all adults;

v) eliminating gender disparities in primary and secondary education by 2005, and achieving gender equality in education by 2015, with a focus on ensuring girls' full and equal access to and achievement in basic education of good quality; and

vi) improving all aspects of the quality of education and ensuring excellence of all so that recognized and measurable learning outcomes are achieved by all, especially in literacy, numeracy and essential life skills.

To achieve all of the goals, quality education must be understood in its widest sense, with education for a culture of peace as an important component of quality education, not only at schools and universities, but also through media, the family and the community as a whole. UNESCO interprets "education of good quality" in the light of the recommendations of the Delors Report[2] which established four pillars of education: learning to be, learning to know, learning to do, and learning to live together. This means that quality education cannot be interpreted solely as academic knowledge. It is an education geared toward building a world based on universal principles of peace and equity, one that develops individuals' ability to protect their dignity as human beings and as citizens, and one that seeks to construct a society in which humanity and citizenship develop to their fullest extent. This also includes efforts to strengthen our education systems and to integrate the struggle against intolerance, prejudice and racism into educational policies.

As such, quality education cannot be limited to people of a certain age or to a certain number of years for, in a changing world, the constant need for adaptation requires an ongoing education that enables the individual, on the one hand, to face the new challenges of his society and, on the other, to re-learn what he or she has un-learned. UNESCO seeks to provide a framework for contributions by all partners to achieve the goal of quality education for all which can serve as a guideline for other actors to conceive, implement and operationalize their projects and harmonize their efforts. Furthermore, the Organization brings its own substantive and concrete contributions for a better adaptation of Member States' education systems and institutions to international norms. This includes renewing curricula, developing educational content and materials, monitoring learning achievement, and encouraging both education for sustainable development and the equitable provision of quality basic education.

The Organization also assists Member States in elaborating and implementing educational policies that promote human rights and responsible and active citizenship by using its expertise for revising educational curricula and textbooks, training teachers and other educational professionals, and producing educational materials, teacher guidelines and training materials. UNESCO promotes an education which advances such notions as universal values, peace and security and informed decision-making. In other words, UNESCO contributes to the establishment of a human rights-oriented quality education in all Member States.

Human Rights

UNESCO's raison d'être, missions and functioning cannot be separated from values. Since its inception, the Organization has served as a central international forum for discussing the ethical, normative and intellectual issues of our time, fostering multi-disciplinary exchange and mutual understanding, working towards universal agreements on these issues, defining benchmarks and mobilizing international opinion.

Human rights constitute the core of these normative principles. They are also a central criterion of a culture of peace as defined by the United Nations General Assembly. Article 1 of the UNESCO Constitution stipulates that furthering universal respect for human rights and fundamental freedoms is among the main purposes for which the Organization was created.

In addition to this constitutional mandate to contribute to the promotion of all human rights, UNESCO has special responsibility with regard to certain rights, in particular the right to education, the right to participate in cultural life, the right to freedom of opinion and expression (including the right to seek, receive and impart information) and the right to enjoy the benefits of scientific progress and its applications. The Organization has also played an important role in the promotion and protection of cultural diversity, which is an ethical imperative inseparable from respect for human dignity and implies a commitment to human rights and fundamental freedoms. Freedom of expression, media pluralism, multilingualism and equal access for all cultures to cultural life, including equal access to knowledge, are all guarantors of cultural diversity and consequently of respect for human rights.

The first step in promoting human rights is to ensure that states and civil society actors understand them. UNESCO has been actively involved in this field in accordance with its Human Rights Strategy – through the promotion of policy-oriented research; the advancement of knowledge, training and information; and standard-setting, monitoring and human rights protection within UNESCO's fields of competence. UNESCO has also established partnerships with various actors and networks, and has concentrated its human rights research on helping Member States and civil society to clarify "the content, nature of obligations, state of implementation, indicators and justiciability of human rights within UNESCO's fields of competence."[3] As part of such a mainstreaming of a human rights-based approach, UNESCO has also contributed to the inclusion of human rights in formal and non-formal educational programmes, and incorporated them in its cultural and scientific activities and guidelines to Member States. UNESCO is equally involved in the monitoring of a number of international normative instruments adopted over the years and in the development of new instruments. For example, UNESCO adopted the Universal Declaration on the Human Genome and Human Rights (1997) as a response to the challenges emerging from progress in research on human genetic data and its resulting applications. The Declaration tries to strike a balance between safeguarding respect for human rights and fundamental freedoms and the need to ensure freedom of research. It states that research and treatment shall be carried out in full respect of human dignity and that no one shall be the subject of discrimination on the basis of genetic characteristics.

Fostering democratic participation is both a human rights imperative and a domain of action for the establishment of a true culture of peace. As a result, UNESCO has been active in promoting participatory democracy, most notably by supporting freedom of expression throughout the world. In a globalized world, the construction of the future cannot be dissociated from communication. If freedom of expression does not exist for political or material reasons, we cannot hope for a multilateral world, since many actors would be voiceless, unable to communicate, hence unable to participate in the making of the future.

Over recent decades, the Organization was able to contribute to the adoption of a number of key regional texts aimed at fostering free, independent and pluralistic media, which were subsequently endorsed by all Member States.

Along with the guidelines provided by these texts, UNESCO has been sensitizing governments, parliaments and other decision-making bodies to legal and practical guarantees of the free flow of information. It has been concurrently offering its technical and legal expertise to respond to Member States' requests for adapting their media laws to international norms while assisting media organizations in drawing up their legal statutes. These activities should be put in the perspective of a larger framework that takes into account the central role of independent media in democratization and reconciliation, and recognizes the negative effects of hate-inciting and warmongering propaganda.

The Organization, therefore, has supported, and continues to support, independent media in zones of conflict. In former Yugoslavia, Rwanda and Afghanistan, for example, the Organization has actively contributed to capacity-building and the promotional efforts of regional media, in close cooperation with other United Nations bodies and professional organizations. Furthermore, acknowledging that community-based media ensure pluralism, diversity of content and the representation of a society's different groups and interests, UNESCO's Community Media Programme provides a framework for cooperation with professional organizations in promoting community-based media, most notably radio stations, which have the advantage of being widely accessible and cost effective.

Gender Equality and Peace

The gap between the rights and status of men and those of women is among the oldest and most pronounced divisions in all human societies. In this regard, UNESCO's ultimate objective is to strengthen the Organization's ability to create the conditions for women and men alike to enjoy human development and security, and to build societies where women and men can reach their full human potential and participate in the development of their societies, sharing its wealth and benefits on the basis of parity. The UNESCO Medium-Term Strategy for 2002–2007 requires the mainstreaming of gender equality in all sectors of UNESCO. This means that, at the institutional level, UNESCO is engaged, with the support of national institutions, in forging and strengthening the political will to achieve gender equality and equity, integrating a gender perspective into all phases of its programme cycle, and using sex-disaggregated data indicators to monitor policies and implement programmes that have explicit gender objectives.

In this quest for gender equality, we must not forget the invaluable contribution of women to peace. One fundamental aspect of UNESCO's work on a culture of peace has been to highlight women's contribution to conflict resolution and reconciliation and to promote a women's vision of peace. In recent years, the role of women in peace-building has been increasingly recognized. One of the greatest steps forward in this area was the unanimous adoption of Security Council resolution 1325 on "women, peace and security" on 31 October 2000. In the years to come, examples of UNESCO's work will include the promotion of affirmative action policies for women in the judiciary in Latin America and women's studies centres in Asian universities. It will also establish a research and documentation centre on women's rights in Palestine, conduct research on women's peace-building efforts and political participation in Central Africa, and analyze women's role in the judiciary and higher education in the Middle East.

Cultural Diversity

UNESCO has a firm commitment to preserve pluralism because development requires interaction and exchange, which in turn require heterogeneity. It is therefore our duty to future generations to preserve our differences in a world that is becoming smaller by the day and, at the same time, to prevent our diversity from becoming a source of conflict. In order to provide the world community with a larger framework, UNESCO has elaborated a normative and practical apparatus that allows and encourages cultural diversity. Chief among these instruments is the UNESCO Universal Declaration on Cultural Diversity, adopted unanimously by the General Conference at its 31st session on 2 November 2001. Aimed at allowing a more vibrant interaction among cultures, the Declaration raises cultural diversity for the first time to the rank of "common heritage of humanity" and responds to two major concerns: first, to ensure respect for cultural identities and, second, to contribute to the emergence of a favourable climate for the creativity of all.

The central challenge relating to cultural diversity is to enable societies, communities and individuals to make their own political and cultural choices in accordance with their specific situations, which are different and change over time. To respond with more impact to this commitment to the protection of cultural diversity, UNESCO is moving to a higher level of standard-setting action by drawing up a binding legal instrument, whereby States Parties to it would take up both rights and obligations to promote and protect the diversity of cultural contents and artistic expressions.

What makes us different today is to a large extent our different pasts, and if we were disconnected from these different pasts our future would be in danger of losing its dynamic character. Keeping in touch with the past, however, means neither being imprisoned by it, nor freezing societies in a given state. It means building the future freely. It means having a foundation on which to build our future.

That holds true for individuals and for peoples, who find in their heritage – natural and cultural, tangible and intangible – the key to their identity and the source of their inspiration. Hence the protection of tangible and intangible cultural heritage contributes to this on-going process of learning from our past to better prepare our future.

To this end, the Organization has launched a number of safeguarding campaigns and operational projects. In particular, these projects are designed to protect the tangible heritage from conflicts and to avoid the destruction of invaluable cultural sites for reasons of symbolism, identity, aggression, misunderstanding and rejection. This work is geared towards restoring the historical and cultural bonds between populations through joint involvement in the protection and preservation of tangible heritage. Cultural heritage encompasses not only magnificent temples but also living culture and its numerous forms of expression. Since the adoption in 2003 of the Convention for the Safeguarding of the Intangible Cultural Heritage, UNESCO has acquired a new and fundamental instrument to help it protect cultural heritage in its entirety at the national and international levels. This instrument will be key for the recognition of human creativity throughout history as a fundamental contribution to the progress of humankind.

Sustainable Development

Another major aspect that we should acknowledge, if we are to create a better future for our children and to achieve the objectives of sustainable development, is our ever-increasing worldwide interdependence. This means recognizing a collective responsibility for the creation of ethical and peaceful societies, including the relations between human societies and the natural environment.

There can be few more pressing and critical goals for the future of humankind than to ensure steady improvement in the quality of life for current and future generations, in a way that respects our common heritage. Education as the foundation of sustainable development was embodied in Chapter 36 of Agenda 21 of the Rio Summit (1992) and this was reaffirmed and further developed at the World Summit on Sustainable Development in Johannesburg (2002). The United Nations General Assembly reaffirmed this essential principle by declaring the period 2005–2014 as the United Nations Decade of Education for Sustainable Development and by designating UNESCO as lead agency for the promotion and international coordination of the Decade. Therefore, the Organization is engaged in the promotion of a global vision of education for sustainable development which embraces environmental protection, economic development and social and cultural development.

The Decade reinforces several long-term endeavours of the Organization. In the field of environmental sustainability, the International Hydrological Programme and the Man and the Biosphere (MAB) Programme constitute flagship projects in the way they address at the same time purely environmental aspects and the interaction between societies and their environment, including through the promotion of greater and stronger cooperation between countries on these issues. The MAB programme identifies biosphere reserve zoning in which conflicts of interest can arise between populations. This implies recognizing the needs of the different populations involved and negotiating with them in order to create a peaceful environment for the conservation and sustainable management of natural resources, wildlife and archaeological heritage. The International Hydrological Programme studies the role of water resources management for sustainable development and the adaptation of the hydrological sciences to cope with the expected changing climate and environmental conditions and, at the same time, integrate the developing countries into worldwide ventures of research and training.

While these efforts are relevant to all the challenges of sustainability, they address more specifically the challenge of resource sharing, primarily from the point of view of governments, and developing decision-making and conflict prevention tools for the future. The underlying concept here is that, although shared resources can be a source of conflict, their joint management should be strengthened and facilitated as a means of co-operation between various stakeholders.

Dialogue among Cultures and Civilizations

Learning to live together – in peace – requires creating spaces for dialogue. In this context, the United Nations and UNESCO have reinforced action in the area of a dialogue among cultures, peoples and civilizations. Overall, the Global Agenda on the Dialogue among Civilizations adopted by the UN General Assembly in its resolution 56/6 at the end of the United Nations Year for a Dialogue among Civilizations (2001) has provided inspiration and a common framework for future action.

The Global Agenda states that dialogue among cultures and civilizations is a process aimed at attaining justice, equality and tolerance in people-to-people relationships. The objective of the dialogue among civilizations is to bridge the gap in knowledge worldwide about other civilizations, cultures and societies; to lay the foundations for dialogue based on universally shared values; and to undertake concrete activities.

As a follow-up, UNESCO, with many partners, organized a series of conferences, meetings, and colloquia in various parts of the world. Dialogue among civilizations – along with the hopes associated with it – was thus revisited and updated. UNESCO's action is also based on Resolution 31C/39 of its General Conference which calls for "international cooperation to prevent and eradicate acts of terrorism". This resolution emphasized that a commitment to dialogue among cultures and civilizations is also a commitment to fight terrorism. It noted that terror rests always and everywhere upon prejudices, intolerance, exclusion and, above all, the rejection of any dialogue.

First and foremost, however, the Organization's many-faceted dialogue activities are guided by resolution 32 C/47, which sets out the framework for concrete and practical activities in the area of dialogue among cultures and civilizations in the domains of expertise of UNESCO. In fact, the Organization has recently introduced three significant new modifications into its approach and practice. The first is a focus on regional and sub-regional levels, as this allows the development of more concrete activities. The second is the focus on thematic issues, such as education or culture. The third is the involvement of a broad range of stakeholders beyond the traditional actors such as governments.

Overall, dialogue among civilizations and cultures has a tremendous capacity to facilitate a culture of peace by strengthening human rights, democracy and tolerance. Dialogue is critical to convey a realistic picture of the diversity of inter-cultural relations. In this context, it is crucial to reconcile the promotion of common universal values with cultural diversity, and to highlight the importance of education both as a basis of a culture of peace and tolerance, and as a crucible of development and poverty alleviation.

United Nations Educational, Scientific and Cultural Organization

Building Knowledge Societies

Ignorance of the Other's way of life, values and heritage, ignorance of the equal dignity of the human being in all cultures and civilizations, and ignorance of the unity of humanity and of commonly shared values can only be countered by creating knowledge societies, so as to enhance the "capabilities to identify, produce, process, transform, disseminate and use information to build and apply knowledge for human development."[4]

However, what can the concept of a "digital revolution" or "knowledge societies" mean to 80 per cent of the world's population who have no access to basic telecommunication facilities, or to the approximately 800 million illiterate adults, or to the two billion inhabitants who still have no electricity? UNESCO is taking an active part in a range of international initiatives to bridge the digital divide that separates rich countries from poor countries and privileged groups from underprivileged groups within the same country, particularly in response to the Millennium Development Goals and the two phases of the United Nations World Summit on the Information Society (WSIS) in Geneva (December 2003) and Tunis (Nov. 2005).

UNESCO is convinced that the new technological advances should be viewed as a means to develop knowledge societies rather than as an end in themselves. Increasing the flow of information is not enough to ensure full access to the knowledge required for development and poverty eradication. Regarded as a driving force of societal change, knowledge now plays a predominant role in all human activities. It has become so strategic that the concepts of development and progress must be redefined in terms of the capacity to create, master, use and transmit knowledge. For UNESCO, the building of equitable knowledge societies rests on four key principles: freedom of expression, access to quality education for all, respect for cultural and linguistic diversity, and universal access to information and knowledge. All these principles have been strongly supported throughout the WSIS process.

*   *   *

The configuration of our world has been changing rapidly in the past few decades and this has created multiple interrelated global challenges and threats. This new configuration, however, also brings with it an unprecedented number of new opportunities for improvement in our living conditions, for the nourishment of the "humanity within human beings" and for greater unity among us. Today, we have more opportunities than ever to come into contact with each other, to learn from one another, to understand each other and, in so doing, comprehend, appreciate and cultivate the very essence of our common humanity. Such progress, however, is conditioned by our willingness to overcome our many prejudices, to accept differences and apply universal principles to what we do individually and collectively. We need to realize that because a common humanity binds us together, progress requires and implies walking the walk together, in solidarity and with respect – in short, fulfilling the vision of a true global culture of peace.

1   A/RES/53/243, Declaration and Programme of Action on a Culture of Peace

2   Learning: the Treasure Within.
     Report to UNESCO of the International Commission on Education for the Twenty-first Century (1996) ce.
     Part A: Declaration on a Culture of Peace (New York, 1999), article 1 (a)

3   UNESCO Doc. 32 C/57 para. 22

4   Communiqué of the Ministerial Round Table on "Towards Knowledge Societies"
     held at UNESCO on 9–10 October 2003.

UNITED NATIONS
DEPARTMENT OF ECONOMIC AND SOCIAL AFFAIRS
– UNITED NATIONS SECRETARIAT –

The Department of Economic and Social Affairs of the United Nations Secretariat is a vital interface between global policies in the economic, social and environmental spheres and national action. The Department works in three main interlinked areas: (i) it compiles, generates and analyses a wide range of economic, social and environmental data and information on which States Members of the United Nations draw to review common problems and to take stock of policy options; (ii) it facilitates the negotiations of Member States in many intergovernmental bodies on joint courses of action to address ongoing or emerging global challenges; and (iii) it advises interested Governments on the ways and means of translating policy frameworks developed in United Nations conferences and summits into programmes at the country level and, through technical assistance, helps build national capacities, including to respond to new challenges such as globalisation.

The outcomes of the UN conferences and Summits of the 90s, the Millennium Summit, the Monterrey Conference and the Johannesburg Summit of the early 2000s provide the comprehensive framework that guides the Department's work in assisting the international community to bring about an enabling environment geared towards poverty eradication, sustained economic growth and sustainable development. The Department promotes the integrated and coordinated implementation of and follow-up to the plans, strategies, programmes or platforms of action agreed to at the UN conferences and Summits to achieve policy coherence at national and international levels.

The Department's policy advisory services are coordinated with the activities of other programmes, funds and entities of the United Nations at the country level within the context of the United Nations Resident Coordinator System and the United Nations Development Assistance Framework. DESA is also the designated organizational liaison for the accreditation of non-governmental organizations (NGOs) in the economic and social areas.

In recent years, new challenges, such as the disparate impacts of globalization, have arisen for international cooperation for development. It has also become clear that immediate political and humanitarian problems should not be allowed to draw attention away from long-term development objectives, and that the international community will only be able to find durable solutions that will prevent reoccurrence of conflicts by addressing the root economic and social causes of conflict. DESA has responded by integrating conflict prevention and peace-building into several areas of its activities. Today the Department is servicing the ECOSOC Ad Hoc Advisory Groups on African Countries Emerging from Conflicts, participating in mechanisms as the Framework Team; mainstreaming gender and bringing gender perspectives to the center of peace processes, strengthening technical cooperation activities for capacity building at the country level in conflict prevention and peace-building, addressing the inter-relationship between social integration and peace-building; and analyzing the impact of conflict on natural resource management and the relationship between natural resource endowments and causes of conflicts.

DESA's publications include major recurrent surveys, such as the World Economic and Social Survey, yearbooks, manuals, guidelines and periodicals.

Contact Information

Office of the Under-Secretary-General

Department of Economic and Social Affairs
United Nations

2 UN Plaza Room 2320
New York, NY 10017
USA

Telephone: + 1 212 963 5958
Fax: + 1 212 963 1010
Email: esa@un.org

Internet: **www.un.org/esa**

Multidimensionality of Peace and Development: a DESA Perspective

José Antonio Ocampo, Under-Secretary-General
for Economic and Social Affairs, United Nations, New York

"Peace, development and justice are all connected to each other.
 We cannot talk about economic development without talking about peace.
 How can we expect economic development in a battlefield?"

Aung San Suu Kyi, Nobel Peace Prize, 1991

One of the major challenges that the United Nations faces today lies in its global task of preventing conflicts and restoring peace through resolution of the causes leading to violent conflict. Today, conflicts are primarily intra-state, protracted and increasingly complex in nature. They mostly occur in the poorer countries of the world, where the development imperative is greatest. More than fifteen of the twenty poorest countries in the world have had a major conflict in the past one and a half decades. Significantly, more than fifty percent of conflicts have recurred and peace agreements broken down within the first decade of achieving peace. Most victims of such civil conflict have been the civilian population rather than parties involved in conflict. The average cost of a civil conflict in a developing country is about US$ 64 billion – exceeding the average annual Official Development Assistance of US$ 62 billion in the 2000s. The impact of internecine civil conflicts has been devastating not only in the conflict affected countries but their spill-over to neighbouring countries has been equally serious. Not surprisingly, therefore, armed conflicts have become a major impediment to economic and social development and sustained peace in many countries. Not only have they reversed development, but the burden of their impact is felt for long years after peace has returned and the work of recovery started. Though conflicts tend to reverse development, in many ways, lack of development itself constitutes a powerful source of grievance fuelled by a combustible mix of poverty, inequality, marginalization and exclusion that often precipitate into violent conflagrations.

Integrating conflict prevention, peacebuilding and development: key United Nations actors

Recognizing the causal interrelatedness between peace and development, the United Nations has taken several steps in resolving conflicts, rehabilitating conflict-affected countries and assisting them in rebuilding their economies and restoring them on the development path. The Security Council, which is the principal organ of the United Nations responsible for the peaceful settlement of disputes and maintaining peace has progressively been integrating development with both peacekeeping and peace-building. At the peacekeeping stage, the primary development focus of the United Nations' activities has been addressing the immediate reconstruction needs. In the subsequent peacebuilding stage, the stress has been on long term development and resolution of the structural causes of conflict. Other principal organs of the United Nations, dealing with economic, social, human rights and humanitarian issues i. e. the General Assembly, ECOSOC and its Functional Commissions, have also been increasingly integrating peace and development issues in their legislation and deliberations.

Within the United Nations Secretariat, relevant departments have been addressing peace and development in a more holistic and integrated manner. For example, the Department for Peacekeeping Operations (DPKO) and the Department of Political Affairs (DPA) have increasingly been addressing socio-economic and developmental issues along with enforcement of peace and security. Similarly, DPA has increasingly been integrating development, human rights and humanitarian issues in its political analyses. The United Nations Development Programme (UNDP) is actively involved in crisis prevention, early warning and conflict resolution and recovery. In cooperation with other departments, the Department of Economic and Social Affairs (DESA) has also undertaken several policy initiatives and actions to address the nexus between peace and development. In addition to these departmental efforts, several inter-agency processes have brought together various UN actors in order to develop a more comprehensive and coordinated approach to conflict prevention. Examples of these are the Interdepartmental Framework for Co-ordination on Early Warning and Preventive Action ("Framework Team") and the Informal Group on the Political Economy of Armed Conflicts.

Addressing new threats and challenges

The world today faces new threats and challenges which are increasingly becoming more interconnected and multidimensional. In recognition of this, the Secretary-General established a High-Level Panel on Threats, Challenges and Change in the fall of 2003. Its mandate was to assess the efficacy of existing approaches, instruments and mechanisms in the light of new threats and challenges and recommend changes necessary to ensure effective collective action by the international community to address them. The panel's report identifies six clusters of threats with which the world must be concerned now and in the decades ahead:

– Economic and social threats, including poverty,
  infectious diseases and environmental degradation;
– Inter-State conflict;
– Internal conflict, including civil war,
  genocide and other large-scale atrocities;
– Nuclear, radiological, chemical and biological weapons;
– Terrorism;
– Transnational organized crime.

The report emphasizes that development "is the indispensable foundation for a collective security system that takes prevention seriously. It serves multiple functions. It helps combat the poverty, infectious disease and environmental degradation that kill millions and threaten human security. It is vital in helping States prevent or reverse the erosion of State capacity, which is crucial for meeting almost every class of threat. And it is part of a long-term strategy for preventing civil war and for addressing the environments in which both terrorism and organized crime flourish."

The panel's report as well as the Report of the Millennium Project, which was established to review progress and make recommendations on the implementation of the Millennium Development Goals, have informed the Secretary-General's report for the September 2005 high-level Summit of the General Assembly entitled *In larger Freedom: Towards Development, Security and Human Rights for All.*[2] In this report, the Secretary-General has forcefully emphasized that development, security and human rights go hand in hand and must be addressed together. Only by doing so, can the world live in larger freedom – free of fear and free from want. Towards this end, the Secretary-General has made far-reaching recommendations and proposed several reforms, including within the United Nations, which are currently being debated in the United Nations.

Multilateralism redefines power relations by creating collaborative relationships between countries based on participatory principles. It can serve to promote conflict resolution, long-term peacebuilding and capacities of nations to govern themselves in a manner that responds to grievances, removes inequalities and is driven by justice and the rule of law. Contrary to this, unilateral actions often rely on force to attempt to resolve conflicts. This only serves to deepen grievances and harden societal divides that remain fundamental causes of perpetual instability, particularly in fragile nations. On the other hand, multilateralism discourages the use of force and provides the tools necessary to resolve conflicts through peaceful means by, inter alia, public awareness, education, respect for diversity, dialogue, mediation and diplomacy. It encourages nonviolent means of conflict resolution grounded in international law. In an increasingly interconnected world, multilateralism provides a solid foundation for peace, security and development. In the words of the United Nations Secretary-General: "It is in the interest of every country to have international rules and to abide by them. And such a system can only work if, in devising and applying the rules, the legitimate interests and points of view of different countries are accommodated, and decisions are reached collectively. That is the essence of multilateralism and the founding principle of the United Nations."

Understanding the underlying causes of conflict

It is essential to understand the linkages between development in its broadest sense, including human rights, environmental sustainability, good governance, participatory democracy, removal of inequalities and discrimination and gender equality, with peace and security if policies, strategies, programmes and initiatives are to be successful in conflict prevention, resolution and sustained recovery. There is abundant literature today on what causes violent conflict. However, there is no one single explanation or model that provides a complete and satisfactory explanation as to why violent conflicts erupt. Some theorists have argued that societies end up in "structural violence" or live without conflicts depending on the way a society is structured.[3] If they embrace a "security approach" in which those in power have a superior strength to defeat or deter opponents, there is peace but there is also a structural possibility of violence. If societies follow a "peace approach" in which differences are resolved peacefully and to the satisfaction of all parties, the possibilities of structural instabilities and violent conflicts are reduced considerably. Some studies focusing on ethno-political groups and non-state communal groups (Minorities at Risk) argue that conflicts most often occur when basic human needs, e. g. the need for physical security and well-being, communal or cultural recognition, participation, and distributive justice are repeatedly denied, threatened, or frustrated, especially over long periods of time. Some analysts, basing themselves on this "Needs Theory" have argued that a primary cause of protracted or intractable conflict is the unyielding drive of people to meet their unmet needs at the individual, group, and societal level. These "needs" require to be fulfilled simultaneously and in an intense and relentless manner.[6]

Researchers attempting to connect violent conflict and poverty have found that conflict, particularly recurring conflict causes poverty[7], but the reverse relationship is not as clear. In many cases, when poverty coincides with ethnic, religious, language or regional boundaries, underlying grievances can explode into open conflict, often triggered by external shocks (such as sudden changes in the terms of trade) or mobilized by groups or individual who are able to benefit, directly or indirectly, from conflict. In this context, transient poor, i. e., those who move in and out of poverty, are particularly prone to the building up of grievance that can lead to violent conflict due to their relatively greater deprivation.

Several recent empirical studies of civil wars have produced crucial conclusions on the links between inequalities and violent conflicts.[8] These studies conclude that vertical inequality does not, ipso facto, increase the risk of internal armed conflicts. Since violent conflicts are primarily group organized conflicts, horizontal inequalities (systematic inequality between groups formed on the basis of ethnicity, language, religious, geographic or other lines) are significantly related to intrastate armed conflict. These studies have found that not only is it important to be aware of the group boundaries of horizontal inequalities, but that it is also important to recognize that inequality itself is a strong cause of grievance that may include political, social, economic, and cultural dimensions.[9] Others studies have found that although every society has motives or grievances, not every group in a society has the opportunity to launch a violent conflict and sustain it. Greed and opportunity provide this ability. These studies also point towards greed being a stronger cause for conflict than grievance.[10]

As can be seen, there are myriad factors that can have a causal relationship with the occurrence of violent conflicts. And these structural causes of conflicts are complex, inter-linked, multidimensional, and often intertwined with a society's history. No one single cause explains the underlying socio-economic causes of conflict fully nor does a single prescription or remedy apply. Therefore, it is critical that each conflict situation or a situation with the potential to erupt into violent conflict be fully analyzed in order to reach an in-depth understanding of situation-specific structural causes that can help to develop sound prevention and resolution strategies. However, while situation-specific causal analysis is critical, there are certain common features of conflict situations that should be borne in mind when formulating strategies and programmes:

– Conflicts exist in all societies and rarely erupt into violence suddenly or without warning;
– There is a differential impact of conflict on women and men, and women can play a vital role in peace building;
– The long-term precursors of violent conflict invariably involve ill-considered governmental policies, inequitable development, social exclusion/marginalization, deteriorating economic conditions and overall institutional decay;
– The international community's security and development sectors need much earlier and more robust coordination to address the underlying causes of conflict so as to forestall the social and institutional disintegration that often leads to violent civil strife;
– The internal dynamics of conflict situations are best understood and can best be addressed by locally conceived and domestically driven solutions that encompass a broad array of inter-linked social, political, economic, security and governance dimensions;
– External assistance must build on, rather than substitute, national capacities, resources and initiatives, using local ownership and building on in-country experience;
– Complex, unique and highly combustible combinations of ethnic/religious differences, economic hardship, and ineffective governance are present in many developing countries. Yet, the actual eruption of destructive conflict depends largely upon the degree to which government and societal institutions have the foresight, skills and capacity to manage tensions and grievance before they deteriorate to violence.

DESA's role, strengths and activities

Addressing the root causes of violent conflict has been a matter of ongoing concern of DESA. Its role as convener of intergovernmental bodies, promoter of norms, mobilizer of civil society, coordinator of the United Nations Executive Committee of Economic and Social Affairs, and source of subject-specific expertise for Member States and the rest of the UN system give it a valuable comparative advantage in dealing with conflict issues. Drawing on its comparative advantages and its comprehensive mandate in the field of social and economic development, DESA has a pivotal role to play in addressing socio-economic factors that underlie violent conflicts. Its expertise is of particular relevance in identifying and addressing socio-economic and institutional causes of potential conflicts through research, analysis and information sharing with Member States, civil society and other UN entities. Its strength particularly encompasses activities in peace-building and post-conflict rehabilitation through policy analysis and development, capacity building, advocacy and information sharing, including on best practices. In post-conflict situations, DESA has a particular role in developing policy frameworks for the integration of such disrupted economies in the global economic arena.

DESA is involved in global policy analysis, norm setting and assisting inter-governmental bodies. In doing these, DESA's *niche* is drawn from its mandate which gives it unique strengths and advantages, some of which are outlined below.

DESA's activities and initiatives in integrating peace and development are based on its mandate and comparative advantages. As the Secretariat of the ECOSOC, DESA has been providing reports, analyses and substantive content in the follow-up of the United Nations Development Agenda[11] that has, at its core, the internationally agreed development goals emanating from United Nations conferences of the last fifteen years as well as the Millennium Summit. Realizing this agenda is critical for the world to achieve freedom from want and freedom from fear. DESA also provides substantive support to the ECOSOC Ad Hoc Advisory Groups on African Countries Emerging from Conflicts, such as the Groups on Guinea-Bissau and Burundi and the Ad Hoc Advisory Group on Haiti, working closely with DPA, UNDP and other relevant stakeholders. In addition, it participates in inter-agency mechanisms devoted to conflict prevention, such as the "Framework Team" established in 1995. DESA also works to mainstream gender perspectives in peace processes, including conflict prevention, management and resolution, peacekeeping and post-conflict peace-building.

At the country level, it is engaged in strengthening technical cooperation activities for capacity building for conflict prevention and peace-building. In the area of social integration, DESA is developing a conceptual/operational framework: "Social Integration as Peace-building: By, For and With People", which addresses the interrelationship of social integration and peace-building. Interlinkages between natural resources and conflicts are also being addressed through analysis of the impact of conflict on natural resource management and the relationship between natural resource endowments and causes of conflicts. DESA is also involved in mainstreaming conflict prevention in governance and institutional development and in the post-conflict reconstruction of institutions. Conducting population census in a number of post conflict situations is yet another important area of DESA's work. Moreover, DESA is developing on-line tools for information sharing and networking among civil society organizations working in conflict prevention.

Substantive challenges faced by the United Nations in integrating peace and development

Although, DESA's activities undertaken in collaboration with the larger UN system have advanced the integration of peace with development, many substantive challenges remain – challenges related to the inherent difficulties of operationalising the conceptual understanding of the interlinkages among conflict prevention, peacebuilding and development – which the UN system faces. They include the following:

i. Structural causes of conflict are multi-layered and multidimensional and policies for prevention and post-conflict need to address *several issues simultaneously* – horizontal inequalities; poverty, underdevelopment and particularly youth unemployment; weak governance institutions and mechanisms; policies of exclusion and marginalization, and issues connected with governance of natural resources.

ii. Each conflict situation has a *unique set of causes with a unique interplay* among them, making the development of a universal model of both diagnosis and policy difficult. Each conflict situation or fragile society needs to be studied individually and analyzed within its own national context.

iii. Causes of conflicts or fragility of states need to be addressed in a proactive manner. Usually, as empirical studies show, a decade passes before grievance turns into violent conflict. Thus, interventions have to be designed in such a manner that a resolution is found *before* societies come to the brink of violent upheaval. In this context, accurate monitoring and diagnosis of horizontal inequalities, identifying ways to reduce them and strengthening governments' capacities to rectify them, are particularly important.

iv. The focus of economic and social policies aimed at reducing poverty, underdevelopment and unemployment and improving government services and distribution of resources need to be geared to attain *"equality of opportunities"* and even some measure of *"equality of outcomes"* and not merely a *"leveled playing field"*. Such policies should be and perceived to be fair in their processes. Two particular difficulties arise in advising Member States on such policies. The first is more political and relates to sovereignty of states. Designing advice and assistance in a manner that Member States do not perceive them as threats to their sovereignty is a delicate issue. The second difficulty has to do with the fact that preventive policies per se need to be nationally driven and owned. Mechanisms that maintain national ownership of policies and programmes while at the same time are subject to international monitoring is a particular challenge.

v. Long-term prevention requires addressing deep-rooted socio-economic, institutional, and other structural causes that underlie immediate symptoms of conflicts, through the strengthening of the capacity of States. It requires good governance; socio-economic policies which enable equitable distribution of wealth; policies or mechanisms for promoting social integration/foster social cohesion while recognizing, protecting and valuing diversity. Specifically, these include having a sound macro-economic structure, putting in place an effective framework for conflict-sensitive fiscal, trade and external debt policies; timely, adequate and equitable delivery of basic social services; an effective judiciary; a depoliticized and professional security sector; participatory national consultative and legislative structures; regular free and fair elections and mechanisms for consultative processes reaching the local levels. All these require a long-term frame. Sustaining such activities, including through provision of adequate and timely resources, over a *long-term frame* is a critical challenge.

vi. The global economic environment can negatively impact on conflict-prone countries. This is particularly so as poorer countries depend on export of a few primary commodities. An additional problem is that trade regimes of developed countries do not encourage export diversification. In the short term, this makes conflict affected/prone countries particularly dependent on the global economic cycle of a narrow list of commodities, while in the longer term such countries suffer from deterioration in their terms of trade. Over time, these economic constraints cause macro-economic adjustment problems, e. g. sudden depreciation of exchange rates, rising oil/fuel prices, cuts in public expenditure. Such external constraints can have negative consequences on good governance by decreasing public sector revenues, and hindering social integration as economic opportunities are reduced. Unfortunately, efforts to address these global market issues are undertaken in discussions outside of the United Nations, hampering efforts to advance the agenda of integrating conflict prevention in the global market discourse.

Structural challenges faced by the United Nations in integrating peace and development

There has been a prevailing awareness that the United Nations can and needs to do more to integrate peace and development in a more integrated fashion and, in that respect, design policies, initiatives and activities that are synergistically and seamlessly interlinked. A major frustration in this endeavour has been the absence of any institutional platform or body dedicated to conflict prevention, peacebuilding and development. The reason for this is that when the Charter was adopted, inter-state wars were the predominant type of conflict. It could not have been foreseen that intra-state and internecine conflicts would overtake inter-state wars. For this reason, the United Nations was conceived without any institutional mechanism that could address this changed nature of conflicts. This crucial shortcoming has been highlighted by the Secretary-General in his report In *Larger Freedom,* prepared as a framework for the September 2005 Summit. To overcome this and in order to address the several dimensions of peacebuilding at one institutional point, among other measures, the Secretary-General has proposed the creation of a Peacebuilding Commission. This Commission will serve to deal with peace and development in a holistic compact. Member States of the United Nations are currently consulting on these proposals and their outcomes will determine how much the United Nations and its component parts, including DESA, can do to prevent violent conflicts and build sustainable peace with development.

Actions initiated by DESA to overcome the challenges

DESA has began a process of introspection and self-evaluation of its mandate, activities, outputs, gaps, and future direction for which a Task Force on conflict prevention, peacebuilding and development within the Department has been created. This Task Force draws on the membership of several of its divisions dealing with specific thematic facets relevant to the integration of peace and development. The Task Force has been mandated to examine the question of consolidating and deepening the on-going activities of DESA in the area; examining ways to strengthen institutional linkages with other organizations and departments working in this area; and identifying specific initiatives and/or approaches on which DESA could focus in order to deepen its work and contribution in this field. The consultative process of the Task Force has been ongoing and as a part of that process, the Task Force held an Expert Group Meeting at the United Nations Headquarters on 15th November 2004 with participation of a cross-section of experts, from the United Nations, academia, practitioners, and Bretton Woods' institutions.

The Meeting examined several issues and made several far-reaching recommendations. Some of them are reproduced below.

– The interrelationship between underdevelopment and eruption of violent conflicts is deeply complex and requires multidimensional analysis and approaches. DESA's evaluative capacities, analytical strengths and convening power makes it well positioned to contribute to the understanding of the socio-economic causes of conflict, including with regard to specific conflict situations.

– Efforts at preventing conflict and peacebuilding at the national level are important. There is, however, increasing recognition of the need to develop sub-regional, regional and global approaches in which a more conducive global policy framework to enable better integration of conflict-prone and countries emerging from conflict in the global economy is critical. Efforts should be made towards this end by all stakeholders.

– Systemic causes of conflict should be addressed in a more comprehensive manner and policy actions should seek to attain "equality of opportunity" and, as mentioned above, some measure of "equality of outcomes" and be responsive to grievances.

– There is need for translating the conceptual side of conflict prevention and peace-building into operational priority for all UN actors, including DESA.

– Privatization of conflicts, including the growing trend of the business sector involving itself in conflict issues, needs to be arrested and reversed including by engaging the business sector, within the existing conflict prevention fora.

The recommendations of the Expert Group Meeting and the outcomes of consultations provide the United Nations system, including DESA, with important guidance in its work in integrating peace and development.

The road ahead:
making the UN development agenda work for peace and progress

On the road ahead lies the twin task of achieving development while building and maintaining peace. Although these goals are not new for the United Nations, they contain new challenges at the beginning of the 21st century. The complexion of wars has changed. Not only are they more internal, they are becoming more protracted. Spillovers of internal wars are becoming wider with refugees crossing several borders, proliferation of small arms and light weapons in war zones abound, land mines prevent agriculture and daily bread-winning activities, and environmental degradation due to civil wars have become more severe. In the light of this changed complexity of civil wars, the bulwark for peace lies in the comprehensive implementation of the broad development agenda which originated from the commitments and the agreed goals contained in the outcomes of the United Nations conferences and summits of the last fifteen years. Making the development agenda work in the task of peacebuilding, in particular, is important if peace is to be sustained and recurrence of wars avoided. These are the challenges faced by the international community on the road ahead.

United Nations Department of Economic and Social Affairs

1 See *A more secure world: our shared responsibility,* Report of the High-level Panel on Threats, Challenges and Change, United Nations, 2004 (A/59/565).

2 A/59/2005

3 Johan Galtung, 2004, "The Security Approach and the Peace Approach", presented at the World Culture Open on "Building Peace through Harmonious Diversity".

4 This project and dataset is featured in the UNDP Human Development Report 2004: "Cultural Liberty in Today's Diverse World".

5 Abraham Maslow, *Motivation and Personality,* 2nd ed., Harper & Row, 1970.

6 Jay Rothman, 1997, "Resolving Identity-Based Conflict in Nations, Organizations, and Communities", San Francisco, CA.

7 Jonathan Goodhand, 2003, "Enduring Disorder and Persistent Poverty: A Review of Current Knowledge on the Linkages Between War and Chronic Poverty", *World Development,* Vol. 31 No. 3

8 Paul Collier and Anke Hoeffler, 2002, "Greed and Grievance in Civil War", Oxford; Hegre, Gissinger & Gleditsch, 2003. Amartya Sen in *Inequality Reexamined,* Oxford, Oxford University Press, 1992, also argues that inequality must be analyzed in terms of groups, rather than specific individuals, and the focus should be on inter-group variations.

9 Francis Stewart, 2004, "Development and Security: working paper 3", Center for Research on Inequality, Human security and Ethnicity, CRISE, Queen Elizabeth House, University of Oxford

10 Collier and Hoeffler, *op.cit.*

11 See the Report of the Secretary-General to the 2005 high-level segment of the Economic and Social Council (E/2005/56).

12 *Ibid.*

UNITED NATIONS
HIGH COMMISSIONER FOR REFUGEES

UNITED NATIONS
HIGH COMMISSIONER FOR REFUGEES

Establishment

The Office of the United Nations High Commissioner for Refugees – UNHCR – was established on December 14, 1950 by the United Nations General Assembly.

UNHCR is headquartered in Geneva, Switzerland.

UNHCR's Executive Committee currently consists of 68 Member States and of more than twenty Standing Committee Observers.

Executive Head

H. E. Mr. António Guterres, UN High Commissioner for Refugees

Objectives

UNHCR is mandated to lead and co-ordinate international action to protect refugees and resolve refugee problems worldwide.

Its primary purpose is to safeguard the rights and well-being of refugees. It strives to ensure that everyone can exercise the right to seek asylum and find safe refuge in another State, with the option to return home voluntarily, integrate locally or to resettle in a third country.

UNHCR offers protection and assistance to refugees and others in an impartial manner, on the basis of their need and irrespective of their race, religion, political opinion or gender.

In all its activities, UNHCR pays particular attention to the needs of children and seeks to promote the equal rights of women and girls.

In more than five decades, the agency has helped an estimated 50 million people restart their lives. Today, a staff of around 6,540 people in 116 countries continues to help 19.2 million persons.

By virtue of its activities on behalf of refugees and displaced people, UNHCR also promotes the purposes and principles of the United Nations Charter: maintaining international peace and security; developing friendly relations among nations; and encouraging respect for human rights and fundamental freedoms.

Contact Information

UNHCR

Boîte Postale 2500
CH-1211 Geneva 2 Dépôt
Switzerland

Telephone: + 41 22 739 8111
Telefax: + 41 22 731 9546

Internet: **http://www.unhcr.org**

United Nations
High Commissioner for Refugees

H. E. Mr. António Guterres, UN High Commissioner for Refugees

The United Nations High Commissioner for Refugees is mandated by the UN to lead and coordinate international action for the worldwide protection of refugees and the resolution of refugee problems. The primary purpose of the Office is to safeguard the rights and well-being of refugees, guided by the 1951 UN Convention relating to the Status of Refugees and its 1967 Protocol. UNHCR pursues lasting solutions by assisting refugees to return voluntarily to their own country or to settle permanently in another country, both through local integration or resettlement to a third country.

Refugees are defined by the 1951 Convention as persons "who has fled from and/or cannot return to their country due to a well-founded fear of persecution, including war or civil conflict." A refugee is a person who "owing to a well-founded fear of being persecuted for reasons of race, religion, nationality, membership of a particular social group, or political opinion, is outside the country of his nationality, and is unable to or, owing to such fear, is unwilling to avail himself of the protection of that country."

The UN General Assembly has authorized UNHCR's involvement with other populations in need, including former refugees who have returned to their homeland, internally displaced people (IDPs), and stateless persons. By virtue of its activities on behalf of refugees and displaced people, UNHCR also endeavours to promote the purposes and principles of the United Nations Charter, including maintaining international peace and security.

The population displacement which UNHCR addresses is most often caused by conflict. Less frequently, UNHCR and the humanitarian community at large have responded to natural disasters in the same way, assisting groups of people displaced by famine, for example, in the same way as refugees fleeing violence. In many cases, population displacement is forced, a tactic of one or more sides in a conflict.

Most situations where UNHCR intervenes to deliver protection and assistance follow a recognizable pattern. The first phase before a population is compelled to flee is usually characterised by a deteriorating human rights and security situation. Movement and flight occurs in a second phase, when there is actual violence and varying levels of conflict. An urgent humanitarian response may follow the displacement in an immediate, post-conflict phase. If stability holds, the fourth phase witnesses the voluntary return of refugees and displaced. This is when solutions are traditionally found for the largest part of an affected population. Lastly, and often following on the heels of returning refugees or IDPs, comes reconstruction and peace-building, when humanitarian agencies are supplanted by development actors and longer-term initiatives.

Displacement resulting from conflict should be viewed as a cycle rather than a single event. Refugee-related work is often dramatized as an urgent and heroic short-term effort, but the role of emergency assistance and protection must be put into context. Urgent humanitarian aid, however appropriate, cannot prevent either an outbreak or a recurrence of violence, or of displacement. UNHCR attempts to ensure that displacement is not protracted unnecessarily, and to focus on the pursuit of durable solutions. A solutions-oriented mandate calls for an awareness of the full sequence of displacement.

UNHCR's role

UNHCR's experience has shown that addressing the cycle of displacement depends on a proactive approach to durable peace and prosperity. Beyond security, these conditions are what ensure the legal and material rights of individuals or groups.

The Afghan case, which for most of two decades represented the world's largest single refugee group and subsequently the largest organized repatriation in the history of the Office, is an example of prolonged human insecurity and of how a major political and humanitarian emergency has shifted to a more complex development challenge. Government capacity is still very weak after more than 20 years of warfare. State and community roles in meeting human security needs are stretched to the limit in this transitional period.

Awareness of the relationship among the range of factors which impact reintegration – which is integral to the durable peace and prosperity of a community – has led to fundamental changes in the way UNHCR approaches refugee return. Returnees in devastated areas, or in areas where communities continue to be deeply divided, have concrete needs. In the 1980s, UNHCR initiated "quick-impact projects" for emergency, small-scale rehabilitation efforts in areas of return. In the early 1990s, several Cold War-fueled conflicts ended with mediation and peace agreements, leading to the large-scale repatriation of refugees to Cambodia, Mozambique, Namibia and Central America. In each of these operations, UNHCR's involvement reflected a new, broader application of the organization's mandate. UNHCR was actively involved in addressing the needs of returnees for longer periods than before, carrying out a wide range of protection and assistance activities to help people to reintegrate and rebuild their lives. By assisting returning refugees and displaced people as part of a comprehensive programme, UNHCR and the international community seek to ensure their successful reintegration, thereby consolidating the peace process. The resilience and ingenuity of former refugees themselves are one of the greatest assets in overcoming obstacles to return, but this can be enhanced with targeted aid.

Reintegration activities take many forms. UNHCR participates in a wide range of general rehabilitation programmes and in activities aimed at encouraging reconciliation. This has typically included aid to rehabilitate basic infrastructure, such as schools, health clinics, and water supply. Local authorities are helped to reestablish themselves and the rule of law. Although returnee families are targeted for specific aid, such as shelter materials to rebuild their homes, most projects benefit entire communities to avoid creating disparities and exacerbating possible tensions between returnees and neighbours who never left the area.

Beginning with these operations in the 1990s, protection, the cornerstone of UNHCR's mandate, has been interpreted in a broader sense. It is seen not only as access to life saving assistance or status, but also as a means to achieve self-sufficiency. Considerable attention, for example, is given to land access as essential to economic survival in places where the majority of livelihoods depend on farming.

This broader understanding of the importance of the reintegration phase – a community's chance to renew with peace and prosperity – has evolved into what we today call "the 4Rs": repatriation, reintegration, rehabilitation and reconstruction. This reflects the relationship between these efforts which, ideally, begin before refugees start home.

An example of "the 4Rs": Liberia

Following the fall of Charles Taylor's regime and the signing of a peace agreement in August 2003, prospects for the repatriation of several hundred thousand Liberian refugees in neighbouring states improved dramatically. The unwelcoming conditions in their home areas remained unchanged, however. The counties which produced the greatest number of refugees and IDPs – Lofa, Maryland, Nimba and Grand Gedeh – were completely devastated by the 14-year civil war.

Despite the obstacles, an estimated 100,000 refugees returned on their own in 2004 alone while another 8,500 have repatriated with UNHCR's help since the agency began organized returns in October 2004. Many more are still scattered around West Africa – in Guinea, Sierra Leone, Côte d'Ivoire and Ghana, with smaller numbers living in the Gambia, Mali, Nigeria, Libya and Senegal. In all, the Office expects to help 340,000 Liberian refugees to return home by the time the repatriation programme is scheduled to wind down in December 2007. IDPs have made up as much as 25 per cent of Liberia's total population, and they too have begun moving back to home areas. Returns on this scale will place enormous pressure on the meager community resources, making reconstruction and rehabilitation assistance urgent if returns are to be sustainable.

UNHCR's community-based reintegration programme in Liberia supports peace-building and reconciliation in the main return areas of return. Restoring infrastructure and basic services aims to ensure that the goodwill and limited absorption capacity of receiving communities are not overburdened in the delicate post-conflict climate. This is critical to peace-building. By empowering the people to begin rebuilding their livelihoods at the individual and community levels, the project is designed to create a viable environment for returning refugees and IDPs, ex-combatants and receiving communities to cohabit peacefully. Resources are directed chiefly towards shelter and agricultural interventions, emergency rehabilitation efforts which will increase the absorption capacity of receiving communities, and the development of community empowerment projects to promote peaceful co-existence. To date, over 1,100 community empowerment projects have been implemented in the main areas of return in Liberia.

Like all UNHCR operations, political and donor support is critical to the success of the initiative. Some of the efforts in Liberia are targeted for funding by the government of Japan, which has a specific Peace Building Grant Aid. The government of Japan has made important donations to other return operations to promote the protection and empowerment of vulnerable people in keeping with their concept of "human security".

Inter-agency collaboration

Programmes like those in Liberia are essentially efforts to bridge the gap between relief and development. It is an enormously complex task requiring not only donor support but also the concerted efforts of several parts of the UN system. Many agencies have responsibilities for programmes which move a post-conflict country along the continuum from relief to recovery. Even before aid agencies can reach an area, peacekeeping missions may be present on the ground to defend the rights of civilians. Early coordination with development actors, including the Bretton Woods institutions and bilateral donors, is essential to the sustainability of reintegration efforts and the link with longer-term development plans. The challenge is to ensure that all these component parts work effectively together to lay the groundwork for sustainable peace and prosperity.

It is clear that an integrated approach to peace-building incorporating the political, peacekeeping, humanitarian, human rights and development processes and actors is essential. From UNHCR's perspective, the link between peace and security and voluntary repatriation of displaced populations is a single, direct line. Including refugee, returnee and IDP issues in the political processes from the outset has huge potential benefits in terms of confidence building, planning for return and ensuring that refugees are included in reconciliation and national development efforts.

UNHCR has made significant strides towards incorporating its concerns into the larger relief and development framework. There is now a widespread recognition of the link between forced population displacement and endeavours to secure international peace and security. Increased collaboration between UNHCR and the Departments of Political Affairs (DPA) and Peacekeeping Operations (DPKO), in particular, has served to highlight this critical relationship. UNHCR's concern for the safety of returning refugees and displaced persons is increasingly being incorporated in the mandates of peacekeeping missions. The Office has also supported the establishment of a more coherent approach to disarmament, demobilization and reintegration

(DDR), which will be led by DPKO. The two "Ds" cannot be obtained without the "R" for reintegration. Former combatants must be given the prospect of a new life, along with refugees and internally displaced persons.

The proliferation of small arms and landmines has proven to be a persistent destabilizing factor in many countries attempting to emerge from insecurity. UNHCR views DDR as an important tool in preventing the recurrence of conflicts, a perspective shared by key regional organizations such as the African Union. The root causes of conflict and peacebuilding were central themes of an all-Africa inter-Ministerial conference which UNHCR co-chaired in 2004. Participants underlined the importance of effectively dealing with the disarmament, demobilization, reintegration and, adding a second "R" to the process, the rehabilitation of ex-combatants, a top priority to prevent countries relapsing into violence. The conference called for lessons to be drawn from successful experiences in order to strike a balance between ensuring reintegration of former combatants and assistance for civilians who suffered the consequences of war. Participants saw this as crucial to effective reconciliation. Recognizing the linkages between conflict and the material and legal rights of individuals, the conference listed respect for human rights, establishment of the rule of law and good governance, resolution of the underlying causes of communal discord, and, importantly, economic and social development needs of communities as the most effective ways to address the root causes of conflict.

Coexistence

Involving returnees and those in the community who never left a country is the starting point for effective reconciliation work. The objective is to overcome the mistrust and antagonism that may have led to rifts between groups. In 2000, UNHCR piloted programmes in the two situations where relations between communities had most notoriously broken down, leading to large-scale refugee crises:
Bosnia and Herzegovina and Rwanda. These were dubbed "Imagine Coexistence", to indicate a first step on the way to true reconciliation.

In Rwanda, a major problem the program dealt with were the legal ramifications of the genocide. At the time, 125,000 Rwandans were imprisoned on charges of genocide. The government worked to balance the survivors' need for justice with the impossibility of trying all of the accused. The projects were developed at the community level and revolved around an economic activity, implemented through NGOs Oxfam (UK) and the Norwegian People's Aid, and through grass-roots associations. The project worked with groups of widows and women whose husbands were imprisoned on charges of genocide. Local networks met with authorities and representatives of civil society, undergoing peace education and conflict resolution training. Particular attention was given to the role of women in bringing communities together, as they are more outspoken defenders of the human security of the family and community. "Imagine Coexistence" in Rwanda came to a close in 2002 after UNHCR handed over the coexistence network to CARE International.

UNHCR has recognized that despite their active role in the practical aspects of reconciliation, reconstruction and rehabilitation, refugee women are largely absent from peace processes. The approach used by "Imagine Coexistence" in Rwanda is one effort to address this. UNHCR has supported other measures to ensure that the experiences and abilities of refugee women are included at different phases of peace processes. In Guinea and Sierra Leone for example, UNHCR funded the missions of several refugee women to ensure their participation in peace delegations under a Mano River Union initiative in West Africa. The Office has also funded the participation of refugee women at a training session on Leadership for Peacebuilding held in Liberia, and of refugee and returnee women at conferences on Gender-based Persecution in Canada and on Gender Relations in Post-Conflict Transition in Norway, in order to ensure that the perspective of displaced women are taken into account in such fora.

Whenever possible, reconciliation and conflict resolution projects are incorporated into core protection work in the country of origin. In Angola, the NGO Centre for Common Ground (CCG) has worked with UNHCR since 2000 on the design and evaluation of protection projects for IDPs and refugees in several provinces. Beginning in 2003, CCG received UNHCR funds for a project to develop productive working relationships between returnees and local government officials, along with skills in conflict resolution and cooperative problem solving in return communities. The project initially involved two northern provinces. However, given its success, it was expanded the following year to all main areas of return. In all, the programme reached more than 26,000 people.

The specific goals of the programme start with straightforward efforts to make all parties – returnees, security forces and local authorities alike – more knowledgeable about the rights of refugees and returnees. Hundreds of information sessions were carried out for groups of returnees on the topics of human rights, norms of repatriation and returnee rights, and basic conflict resolution techniques. Returnee groups were empowered to act as leaders back home and participate in community decision making. CCG brought together all sectors of civil society to engage in constructive dialogue on issues which surfaced with the repatriation of Angolans following the end of the civil war. National journalists were sensitized to the issues and trained on protection, increasing the capacity of media outlets to promote social dialogue. Radio spots were aired regularly in target areas while purpose-designed theatre performances brought the same messages to audiences of thousands.

The programme was reviewed by independent evaluators at the end of 2004 and results were found to be impressive. The evaluation noted that although training often has little lasting impact, these activities produced demonstrable attitude and behaviour changes which contributed directly to the building of sustainable peace in Angola.

Prevention

Peacebuilding on return guards against the recurrence of conflict and displacement. Prevention activities, largely lacking in current situations, can also take place before refugees even set out for home.

One of the most forward-looking efforts UNHCR has initiated in this area is the Peace Education Programme. PEP was started in 1998 in the camps of Dadaab and Kakuma, housing mainly Somali and Sudanese refugees respectively, in Kenya. The large camps are notoriously combustible, housing mixed populations with little prospect for imminent repatriation. Both are prone to regular conflicts between refugees of different clans and between the refugees and surrounding communities. PEP was begun with the belief that peace can be fostered by promoting changed behaviour and by the practice of specific, teachable constructive skills. The objectives were to enhance the quality of life for individuals, the community and the nation by preventing violent conflict; impart mediation and peace-building skills which would preempt conflict; and offer refugees a new understanding of the value of peace. Peace education was intended to benefit refugees in the short term, while still in exile, and on their return home.

A needs assessment was carried out using participatory workshops, after which a curriculum and methodology were drawn up. The kit developed as a result included culture-specific teachers' and facilitators' guides, trainers' materials, story books, posters, role play and proverb cards. The programme targeted both youth and adults through sessions organized in schools and community workshops. PEP was establis-hed as an education programme rather than a communication-based effort.

As in Angola, an independent evaluation reviewed the experience of PEP to determine how successful it had been and whether any lessons could be applied in other refugee situations. The evaluation, carried out in the Kenyan camps four years after PEP was launched, found ample statistical and anecdotal evidence that the programme had exceeded expectations. Reviewers identified several contributions to camp life and refugee interaction including improved camp security and a drop in crime, contain-ment or resolution of disputes and quarrels, prevention of open conflicts, and more and more positive inter-group integration. Evaluators were able to document tangible con-tributions to peace in the camps and daily demonstrations of non-violent, supportive relations in an atmosphere that was generally rife with confrontations. Refugees who had acquired mediation skills were even called on by the local Kenyan police to help resolve disputes peacefully.

By the time of the evaluation, the positive experiences in the Kenyan camps had led UNHCR offices in four other African countries to adopt the project. In addition, preli-minary training and design planning workshops had been conducted in several others. The school programmes had reached nearly 200,000 school children through the Peace Education curriculum, and the programme has been extended to national secondary schools in Kenya and Liberia.

The PEP is intended to improve the life of today's refugees and to give tomorrow's returnees values which will help prevent a recurrence of the conflict and violence which led to their displacement. It seeks to equip individuals with skills which will help them navigate inevitable disagreements while avoiding physical violence at all costs.

These are examples of efforts to improve the security of communities affected by con-flict and displacement. UNHCR reintegration and coexistence projects attempt to offer protection, in both legal and material forms, to refugee and IDP populations and their communities of origin in the phase when societies can easily backslide into conflict.

Other facets of security

We have seen the implications for peace and security if refugees are not helped to reestablish themselves in their place of origin. Of course, well before that can happen, a country which accepts and hosts refugees has security concerns of its own. Movements across borders impact peace and security. There is a risk that combatants might use the asylum country to regroup and train, or profit from the humanitarian aid intended solely for civilians. The simple act of taking in people trying to escape a conflict may be misunderstood by the warring parties. As a result, many states bordering a country torn apart by civil war, or under threat from another neighbour, naturally fear that hosting refugees will draw them into the conflict.

The prospect of a large refugee influx menacing the security and prosperity of a developed country has been a rare one during the past 50 years. Over the past decade, the number of refugees in the world has declined from around 27 million to 17 million. The drop has come about with the end of several long-running conflicts which subsequently allowed large-scale return to Afghanistan, Bosnia and Herzegovina, and several countries in Africa. Although the vast majority of those refugees had been hosted by neighbouring countries in the respective regions, the impact of the repatriation movements has been felt much farther afield: asylum applications in many European states have dropped steadily during the same period and are currently at their lowest levels in more than 20 years.

Despite this trend, attitudes in many developed countries have hardened towards asylum seekers. One of the most pressing issues UNHCR faces at present is the perception in industrialized nations that refugees pose a growing threat to their security and economies. Refugees are often portrayed for political ends as a threat to the prosperity of a country and its own citizens. In the post-9/11 world, an ever-greater number of developed countries concerned about national security and the fight against terrorism are enacting increasingly restrictive asylum laws. Migratory policies in many countries have been narrowed with the overriding objective of preventing the flow of undocumented migrants and irregular secondary refugee movements. Facing the changed nature of conflict and the effects of globalization, many states have tried to redefine and limit their responsibilities towards refugees.

The politicization of immigration and confusion between refugees and migrants has combined to sour public debate and water down asylum legislation in many states, eroding refugee protection. Within the current security context, it is all the more important that states strive to achieve an appropriate balance. UNHCR recognizes the right of states to control their borders and regulate the entry of foreigners in their territories. The Office is providing substantive assistance to multilateral efforts to preserve asylum space and addressing the stages of displacement from countries of origin through methods of transit. Through the early registration of asylum-seekers, timely protection interventions and reintegration activities that give former refugees a chance to start life over, UNHCR is well-placed to combat irregular secondary refugee movements. In doing so, the Office can be an ally for security.

Support for refugee programmes is in fact an investment in solutions to larger questions, issues such as insecurity and underdevelopment. Refugees are among the most vulnerable people on earth; limits on the protection of human rights of persons moving across borders only make them more so. UNHCR will continue to advocate that strengthened international resolve, rather than new restrictions, are the best guarantee for global peace and security by providing lasting solutions to refugee problems.

WORLD BANK GROUP

WORLD BANK GROUP

Establishment

Conceived during World War II at Bretton Woods, New Hampshire, USA, the World Bank initially helped rebuild Europe after the war. Its loan of $ 250 million was to France in 1947 for post-war reconstruction. Reconstruction has remained an important focus of the Bank's work, given the natural disasters, humanitarian emergencies, and postconflict rehabilitation needs affect developing and transition economies.

Today, the World Bank is a Group, encompassing five closely associated institutions: The International Bank for Reconstruction and Development (IBRD), the International Development Association (IDA), the International Finance Corporation (IFC), the Multilateral Investment Guarantee Agency (MIGA), and the International Center for Settlement of Investment Disputes (ICSID).

The World Bank Group is headquartered in Washington, D. C., USA.

The World Bank Group is comprised of 184 Member States. The Bank is like a cooperative, where its 184 member countries are shareholders.

Executive Head

H. E. Mr. Paul Wolfowitz, President of the World Bank Group

Objectives

Our dream is a world free of poverty

The World Bank Group's mission is to fight poverty and improve the living standards of people in the developing world. It is a development Bank which provides loans, policy advice, technical assistance and knowledge sharing services to low and middle income countries to reduce poverty. The Bank promotes growth to create jobs and to empower poor people to take advantage of these opportunities.

The World Bank Group helps people help themselves and their environment by providing resources, sharing knowledge, building capacity, and forging partnerships in the public and private sectors.

The Bank-supported projects have helped increase education for poor children, reduce tuberculosis infections, fight HIV/AIDS and connect villages in many developing countries.

Contact Information

World Bank Group

1818 H Street, N. W.
Washington, D. C. 20433
USA

Telephone: + 1 202 473 1000
Fax: + 1 202 477 6391

Internet: **http://www.worldbank.org**

Another Name for Peace: Development

Katherine Marshall and Lucy Keough
Development Dialogue on Values and Ethics Unit

Introduction

At the Millennium Summit in September 2000 the member states of the United Nations reaffirmed, through the Millennium Declaration and the subsequent, action focused, framework of the Millennium Development Goals (MDGs), their commitment to a world free of poverty and social injustice. These Goals serve as a vehicle for focusing the efforts of the world community on achieving significant, measurable improvements in people's lives. They are simply stated, mutually reinforcing undertakings with target dates, directed at reducing poverty in all its forms.

None of the Millennium Development Goal speaks directly to conflict, but the linkages between conflict, poverty and development have been amply demonstrated. War is development in reverse, and hence presents a monumental impediment to the eradication of poverty, to the improvement in access to health and education, and the attainment of many of the other MDGs. A diminution of conflict would contribute very significantly to the realization of the MDGs.

It is now some five years since the MDGs were adopted and 2005 has been designated as the "Year of Development." As we look toward a review by global leaders at the United Nations in September of progress toward realizing these goals, the reality is that for many developing nations they remain a distant hope. While some parts of the global economy have benefited from the effects of globalization and economic growth, many other parts have been left behind; they have suffered increased instability and decreased social justice, as a result of violence, instability, and the legacy of conflict. The combined impact of these conditions stands as a persistent obstacle to prosperity and social justice. That 15 of the world's 20 poorest countries today have suffered from a major conflict in the past 15 years bears painful testament to this fact.

The rising incidence of intrastate and civil conflict over the past decade, along with the attendant economic devastation and social tragedy that inevitably result, are now among the most critical development challenges facing many of the world's poorest nations. This paper explores the links between economic development and conflict, and suggests what the appropriate role for the World Bank and other multilateral development organizations might be. Much of the discussion is devoted to civil conflict, since, despite the global attention paid to international conflicts, civil conflicts are far more prevalent and their impact is felt by much larger populations.

As the international community comes to understand the complex relationship between conflict and development, it has become increasingly apparent that conflict is both a cause and consequence of economic underdevelopment, poverty, and social exclusion. When festering tensions flare into violent conflict, years and even decades of development efforts are erased, economic and social institutions are decimated, and poverty becomes more entrenched. Conflict severely undermines the capacity of a nation to support economic development policies, foster social justice, or even sustain the basic conditions of stability. The ultimate result is that nations become trapped in a vicious cycle of violence and poverty.

In light of the links between global security and development, the imbalance in the level of global resources devoted to military expenditures – some $ 1000 billion annually – and development purposes – some $ 65–70 billion – appears staggering.

While the international community has sometimes – though not always – demonstrated a willingness to respond to conflicts with either humanitarian aid or direct intervention, the capacity to prevent conflict – even in the face of obvious tensions likely to degenerate into conflict – and the ability to sustain a durable peace in nations emerging from the ravages of war have remained weak and inconsistent. This is all the more troubling considering that the scale of devastation now caused by civil conflicts has increased dramatically, including staggering increases in mortality and morbidity rates among non-combatants – thought to generally represent about 75 percent of the victims of warfare – widespread human rights violations, and severe economic devastation. The case for international intervention is underscored by the fact that the perpetrators of war are often shielded from its consequences.

Real progress toward the eradication of poverty will hinge critically on incorporating conflict prevention and peace-building into the development agenda, and vice versa – these twin faces of social injustice and inhumanity are inextricably linked. At the core of the Millennium Development Goals is the objective to reduce global poverty by half by 2015. Should some similar commitment be made to reducing the global incidence of civil wars? It is clear that achieving any progress toward the other goals will require a significant reduction in the occurrence of civil wars. Explicitly embracing the goal of reducing civil conflict by half by 2015 could do much to raise awareness within the development community about the linkages between poverty and conflict and the need to establish specific policies to address these challenges.

In recent years, the world has increasingly recognized that poverty is both a cause and a consequence of conflict. Recognizing the relationship between development and conflict is a solid first step. The next step would be to ensure that both conflict prevention and recovery are embedded squarely in the core of the development agenda and factored into the design of countries' development programs and policies. Experience has aptly, often tragically, demonstrated that, as a global community we can no longer blithely pay lip service to the importance of conflict prevention while leaving this at the periphery of development priorities. Instead, development strategies based on equitable growth, increased access and improved quality of health and education services could foster conditions to lessen the likelihood of conflict and help nations emerging from war achieve sustained peace.

The Nexus of Development and Conflict

Historically, civil conflicts were largely assumed to be rooted in long standing and deep-rooted political, social, ethnic, or religious tensions. The economic and development conditions of a nation were seen as merely the background against which these other factors played out. Since violence was seen as an eruption of ancestral, ethnic, or religious hatred, the role the international development community could play in conflict prevention seemed to be severely constrained.

More recent work over the last decade has yielded a better understanding of the underlying factors that contribute to the incidence of civil war. While armed civil conflicts are complex phenomena, with a varied mosaic of distinct and particular ethnic, religious, and historic tensions, often their most fundamental genesis can be traced to an underlying pattern of development failure and economic collapse that transcends traditional, ethnic or religious animosities. Behind the labyrinthine and idiosyncratic triggers which set the tinderbox alight, there is often a common thread of poverty and dwindling economic opportunities.

Weak political institutions and lingering religious and ethnic tensions are well harrowed causes of conflict. Less well understood but equally important is the absence of economic development. It can indeed contribute to the eruption of large-scale violence. This relationship between poverty and conflict is not merely speculative. It has been empirically demonstrated in research which shows that civil wars are heavily concentrated in the poorest countries. Recent analysis of modern civil conflict has revealed that the risk of civil conflict in the poorest countries is 15 times greater than that of middle-income nations. Moreover, the mean per capita GDP in countries which have seen civil war any time between 1960 and 1999 is less than half that of countries which have experienced no civil war, reflecting the fact that countries which have seen civil war have also seen much slower rates of economic growth.[1]

Countries that have stagnant or faltering economies, where per capita incomes remain unequally distributed and economic and social institutions are collapsing under the weight of mass poverty, face a dangerously high risk of conflict. Poverty and unequal distribution of wealth create a pool of impoverished and disaffected young men that present easy "targets" for charismatic rebel groups to be recruited with promises of the spoils of conflict. In such conditions, the state also tends to be weak and non-democratic, lacking the institutional capacity to act as a brake upon the escalation of violence.

History and literature confirm the statistics of modern war – that women and children are deeply affected when conflict rages in the community. Today, however, women are often directly involved in the insidious forms of modern conflict, which persist year after year, penetrate every dimension of social life, and leave a legacy of bitter memory. Children are too often brought into conflict as soldiers, and many more suffer lasting physical and psychological scars of horrors of civil conflict. Conflicts erode every level of human decency and the evidence of widespread rapes and violence against women and children is powerful evidence that this may be worse today than in recent memory. Contrasting with this picture of a society shaped by conflict is a ray of hope, in the many examples of women emerging as peacemakers and taking central roles in shedding light on horrors of conflict but still more helping with the critical tasks of building hope in a decent future.

The Vicious Cycle of Poverty and Violence

Failures of economic development which increase the likelihood of civil unrest is only half of the story. Not only does economic underdevelopment create conditions that accentuate tensions and seed potential conflicts. Civil war also devastates a nation's economic foundations and undermines whatever development progress had been achieved. A nation attempting to transition from civil war to peace is at a high risk of returning to conflict because some key conditions that led to the initial outbreak of violence have worsened. Typically, a country reaching the end of a civil war faces over a 40 percent risk of relapsing into violence.[2] Civil war not only interrupts, but actually reverses, economic progress.

By the end of the typical civil war, incomes are reduced by about 15 percent, which translates into about 30 percent more people living in absolute poverty. Not only are more people impoverished, but the effort needed to improve the situation is much greater than had a war never occurred, because physical infrastructure has been destroyed, government services are almost always negligible, economic institutions have crumbled, and corruption is often rife.

Contributing to this economic fallout is that much of a country's financial and human resources are diverted during conflict from productive activities toward the destructive activities of the war effort. Military expenditures are increased, with a commensurate decrease in resources available to support social service delivery, infrastructure development or economic growth. Both men and women may be drawn into combat and thus can no longer participate as productive members of the economy. In these ways, a country engaged in a civil war loses vast amounts of available capital that should have been promoting economic development and reducing poverty.

The impact of this diversion of resources is actually compounded by the fact that these resources are used for destructive purposes, thus constituting a double loss: the loss of the social programs and economic benefits previously supported by such resources, plus the actual losses resulting from the conflict-caused damage. The most obvious damage caused is the direct destruction of infrastructure. During civil war, forces target vital strategic physical infrastructure such as telecommunications, airports, ports, roads, and bridges. In addition, forces – on both sides – often loot and destroy housing, schools, and health facilities. This type of destruction seriously impedes economic growth and undercuts the development process.

Along with this diversion of resources and destruction of economic infrastructure, capital flight also heavily contributes to the economic impacts of conflict as concern over a nation's stability will almost inevitably cause investors – foreign or domestic, whether they be individuals, corporations, governments, lending agencies, or financial institutions – to shift their assets elsewhere and to be overly cautious about future ventures since the post-conflict landscape will be marked by the fear of conflict relapse. The ultimate result is that the financial resources available for productive activities dry up. Even after the conflict has ended, this persistent insecurity substantially hampers post-conflict reconstruction and the potential for sustainable growth.

Conflict Prevention, Peace-Building and Development

Since the end of the Cold War, there has been a marked increase in the global incidence of civil conflict which has plagued many of the world's poorest countries and wrought horrendous tragedy upon the world's most vulnerable people. However, the passing of the Cold War meant the end of superpowers playing out their rivalries using developing countries as proxies. This has created new opportunities for more effective international efforts toward conflict resolution and peace-building. The opportunity now exists for the partnerships in the development community becoming relevant players in conflict prevention and broader peace-building processes.

Where economic development programs have failed, where people are unemployed and have no access to basic social services, and where people have no stake in the economic system, there is a persistent risk of violent conflict. But conversely, where there is greater equity in the distribution of resources, where people have access to basic services and employment opportunities, and where people therefore have a real stake in the economic system, the risk of violence is reduced. Whereas conflict precludes development, so development can preclude conflict. This growing awareness of the relationship between economic development and conflict compels two further realizations: first, that appropriately designed and implemented development strategies can have a significant, measurable impact in easing tensions before they degenerate or relapse into violence; and second, that the development community has a responsibility to take a more active and effective role in conflict prevention and peace-building.

Priorities for the Development Agenda

The transition from war to peace, when peace is still very fragile, needs to show rapid and material progress and is thus a critical period for international support and assistance. Strategies and policies for recovery and rehabilitation should be appraised on the criterion of their impact in either mitigating or aggravating the risk of a relapse of conflict. Certain combinations of characteristics can make a country radically less prone to violent conflict. Reviving economic growth should be a top priority of any post-conflict agenda. Economic policies in the initial phases of post-conflict transition need to aim at the reduction of poverty, improved social services and the rebuilding of war-torn communities in the context of overall equitable economic growth. An important aspect of growth policies should be reducing reliance on exports of primary commodities whose prices are highly volatile. Episodes of price crashes may induce the growth collapses that increase the risk of conflict. Countries with a more diversified economic base are more resilient to adverse shocks and hence less susceptible to such destabilizing forces.

Social policies should be designed around the objective of inclusion. Key aspects include the demobilization of ex-combatants, the reintegration of refugees, the removal of land mines, all of which are critical to the consolidation of peace. Programs and policies in this regard need to show special sensitivity to the needs of women and children, particularly returning child and female soldiers.

A key policy priority is the reduction of corruption. Where revenues are embezzled by narrow elite rather than used transparently for the public good, rebel movements are emboldened and the risk of conflict rises. Governments therefore have a strong interest in demonstrating that revenues from natural resources, foreign aid, and tax revenues are used in an appropriate manner and for the material benefit of all. Reducing corruption not only increases the perception that the government is acting on behalf of the people, it also provides the government with greater resources for implementing its economic policies and delivering social services. Both of these benefits significantly contribute to reducing the likelihood of violence.

The sustained support from international community plays a vital role in recovery efforts. When global attention is caught by a new cause, humanitarian assistance and financial aid can dwindle. In the immediate aftermath of war, international publicity and goodwill is considerable, and so donors are keen to be involved in humanitarian relief efforts. Unfortunately, it is too often the case that donors curtail the flow of aid after three or four years of post-conflict reconstruction, just a country has begun to rebuild its basic infrastructure and reconstitute its financial institutions, when both the need for sustained support is great and so is the capacity to utilize it effectively. This type of sustained aid can significantly contribute to economic growth and help cement a lasting peace.

Reaching out to Non-Traditional Actors

Development institutions, including the World Bank and other international financial institutions, cannot resolve conflicts. They neither carry nor seek a mandate for peace-making or peacekeeping. In fact, many aspects of peace mediation are quite specifically prohibited to them. Other organizations have assumed that mantle: the United Nations, national diplomatic services and a host of non-governmental and civil society organizations founded for this purpose. Within this group, faith based organizations constitute an increasingly important constituency. The increasing recognition of the inter-linkages between conflict and development has made these issues central in the development agenda.

Partnerships among the myriad institutions – and reaching out to non-traditional actors – engaged in conflict prevention and resolution holds great promise for supporting the prevention of violence and transition from war to a consolidated peace. Taking advantage of synergies and complementary experience and capacities, building bridges between various types of organizations can, together, provide a package of appropriate assistance and technical interventions that can help to remove some of the core impediments to reconstruction and a firmer base for socially sustainable development.

Among these, faith based organizations merit special mention. Faith organizations have repeatedly demonstrated a stalwart commitment in the face of conflict. Many remain active and "on the ground" irrespective of personal danger. In many conflict areas, where government services have ceased to exists, whether because of on-going conflict or isolation or remoteness, faith based organizations have frequently remained the sole source of education and heath services. In some war torn countries, it has been said that more children know how to shoot than to read. The contributions of faith groups in providing social services in war zones, especially health and education services, can contribute to the realization of the MDGs in regions which would otherwise have no access to services.

Their engagement in post conflict reconciliation efforts especially at the community level is equally incontrovertible. The prophetic vocation of faith leaders in conflict areas is critical, both at a community level, in providing physical relief and spiritual comfort and at a policymakers' level, in having easy access to decision makers. For groups hovering on the edge of despair and hopelessness, faith leaders can provide succor and relief and solidarity at the front lines. The role for religious leaders and communities is thus, while holding much potential, quite a difficult one.

With notions of justice deeply embedded in all major faiths, religious leaders are uniquely placed to speak out against injustice and inequality between peoples within countries, as an important means of preventing conflict and or paving the way for reconciliation following conflict. Faith leaders can contribute to reconciliation by working to break down walls between different ethnic or religious groups – doing away with distinctions between groups – the "us and them" syndrome which makes one group the adversary.

Recent history abounds with examples of faith leaders and organizations playing central roles in conflict resolution and peace building. There are inspiring stories from Sierra Leone of interfaith cooperation between Muslims and Christians to supply basic needs to war-torn communities irrespective of faith affiliation, which ultimately was a significant factor in rebuilding communities. In Northern Uganda, an almost forgotten conflict which has waged for years, the Acholi Religious Leaders Peace Initiative, organized in 1997 by an alliance of the Catholic Church, the Anglican Church and Muslims in the Gulu and Kitgum districts, has worked tirelessly to promote dialogue between the government and the rebel Lord's Liberation Army. Although the group has seen large measures of both success and failure in its efforts, it persists with unflagging commitment. In Cambodia in 1992, a peace march by more than 100 Buddhist monks and nuns from the main refugee camp for Cambodians in Thailand back across the border symbolized that peace was returning, step by step. Since then other faith based initiatives have helped to rebuild Cambodian society, illustrating the importance of attending to the grass roots power or religion even when conflicts are not rooted in religious tensions.

Among the best known faith based groups working in conflict resolution is the Community of Sant'Egidio. A Catholic lay association founded in the late 1960s on a determination to work with very poor communities, Sant'Egidio is perhaps best known for the key role it played in mediating the peace process in Mozambique. Employing a "two track negotiation" process at national and international levels, its contribution was widely recognized as pivotal to the resolution of this long standing conflict. Sant'Egidio has engaged in other efforts to rebuild communities shattered by conflict and to combat the more durable and intractable problems of poverty. Sant'Egidio brings together in a seamless continuum a powerful focus on peace and a continuing concern and advocacy for the very poor. They have earned a special status for their work in poor and conflict-ridden countries in different parts of the world, widely recognized for its deep commitment and its skill and experience.

In two specific cases, Sant'Egidio has partnered with the World Bank. First, in Central Albania, Sant'Egidio collaborated with the World Bank in 1998 on a program aimed at responding to the regions' enormous education and health needs following the arrival of refugees from the north. The project aimed to strengthen health and educational services, increasing resources for school and drug supplies and for training of local personnel. The intervention proved to be very timely and moved quickly, because the Community of Sant'Egidio was already present in Albania and Kosovo. The synergy with the World Bank funding added to the rapidity and effectiveness of the intervention. Another important success factor was deliberate collaboration with the local population, ensuring that they were active participants. The intervention played a role in not only preventing possible health problems but also possible discontent and tension between the local population and the refugees. A second joint effort between Sant'Egidio and the World Bank was in Guinea Bissau, where support for rebuilding and reconstruction of a hospital damaged in civil strife was expanded to tie in to a World Bank supported health sector operation. This is an instance where the two institutions learned significant lessons from the other, coming as they did from very different perspectives – Sant'Egidio from the position of a damaged hospital needing rehabilitation, and the World Bank from the perspective of policies and financial and operational needs for the national health system overall.

Conclusion

Economic development is the critical factor in preventing and reducing the incidence of conflict. It is clear that there is a deep interrelationship between development failure and conflict, between economic growth and security. Those nations that suffer from chronic underdevelopment and whose people are living in abject poverty are at a significantly greater risk for civil conflict and violence. On the other hand, however, if those nations can establish the conditions and institutions necessary for real economic growth, there is a greater chance that tensions can be resolved through non-violent channels rather than degenerating into disorder and violence.

There is no simple solution to the chronic underdevelopment that now plagues so many nations and sentences billions of the world's people to a life of poverty. These are complex problems that demand the comprehensive, long-term involvement of many actors, including not only governments and other official public bodies, but also with a special role for increasingly engaged and vibrant civil society organizations, faith communities and the private sector. All must stand shoulder to shoulder in partnership with affected countries to work toward country specific conflict resolution, global security and global poverty eradication. The degree to which the world community succeeds in this goal will have a major bearing on the realization of the Millennium Development Goals.

If the world's poorest countries are to avoid the devastation caused by persistent violence and civil disorder, the international community needs to reorient the development agenda. The world cannot enjoy peace without economic progress, and economic progress is but a dream without lasting peace. We must approach this challenge with vigilance and determination, but also with humility and hope.

1   *Breaking the Conflict Trap: Civil War and Development Policy*, World Bank Policy Research Report,
     World Bank and Oxford University Press, 2003

2   Ibid

WORLD TOURISM ORGANIZATION

WORLD TOURISM ORGANIZATION

Establishment

The World Tourism Organization (WTO), a specialized agency of the United Nations, is the leading international organization in the field of tourism. It serves as a global forum for tourism policy issues and practical source of tourism know-how.

The World Tourism Organization is headquartered in Madrid, Spain.

The World Tourism Organization has 145 Member Countries, and comprises seven territories and more than 300 Affiliate Members representing the private sector, educational institutions, tourism associations and local tourism authorities.

Executive Head

H. E. Mr. Francesco Frangialli, Secretary-General of WTO

Objectives

The World Tourism Organization plays a central and decisive role in promoting the development of responsible, sustainable and universally accessible tourism, with the aim of contributing to economic development, international understanding, peace, prosperity and universal respect for, and observance of, human rights and fundamental freedoms. In pursuing this aim, the Organization pays particular attention to the interests of developing countries in the field of tourism.

The WTO plays a catalytic role in promoting technology transfers and international cooperation, in stimulating and developing public-private sector partnerships and in encouraging the implementation of the Global Code of Ethics for Tourism, with a view to ensuring that member countries, tourist destinations and businesses maximize the positive economic, social and cultural efforts of tourism and fully reap its benefits, while minimizing its negative social and environmental impacts.

Contact Information

World Tourism Organization

Capitán Haya 42
28020 Madrid
Spain

Telephone: + 34 91 567 81 00
Fax: + 34 91 571 37 33

Internet: **http://www.world-tourism.org**

Tourism Helps Strengthen the Peace Process

Rok Klancnik, Director, WTO Press and Communications

It was former US President John F. Kennedy who once said:

"Travel has become one of the great forces for peace and understanding in our time."

"As people move throughout the world and learn to know each other, to understand each other's customs and to appreciate the qualities of individuals of each nation, we are building a level of international understanding which can sharply improve the atmosphere for world peace."

His comments come very close to the statutes of the World Tourism Organization (WTO), which define the Organization's fundamental aim as "the promotion and development of tourism with a view to contributing to economic development, international understanding (and) peace."

This aim was uppermost in the minds of the representatives of our then 137 member countries who voted unanimously to establish a Global Code of Ethics for Tourism at the WTO General Assembly in Santiago, Chile in October 1999.

The Global Code is, without doubt, one of the most remarkable advances made in recent years in world tourism. Some people regarded it then with scepticism, this plan to establish a frame of reference and common standards for all partners in the sector.

But the Code has established a direct link between the liberalization of tourism trade, sustainable development, control of the social and cultural impact of tourism, and the promotion of a culture of peace through tourist exchange. To achieve this, it lays down a set of principles spelling out the rights and obligations of visitors and hosts and, more broadly, of partners in the tourism industry.

The Code, and indeed WTO's work in general, lays special emphasis on the complex relationship between tourism and peace, because tourism can only thrive in a safe and peaceful environment. Any terrorist attack, and tourism to that country is affected.

Tourism in itself is a harbinger of peace, because the direct contact it fosters between visitor and host is irreplaceable. How can anyone feel enmity for someone he has known or received personally? As John Steinbeck once wrote, tongue in cheek, "besides the fact that they leave behind their economies wherever they go, I believe tourists are very useful to the modern world: it is very difficult to hate the people one knows".

Also, the destinations and tourism operators in a given region are bound by a common destiny and a common interest in shared development projects: why confront each other when peace profits everyone and conflict no one?

History has shown that the forces unleashed by tourism are so powerful that they can change apparently irreversible situations and bring about reconciliation where none was considered possible.

Who would have thought, at the beginning of the 1970s, that tourism would radically change the economic structure and political system of countries such as Spain, Portugal and Greece and make them some of the world's most popular holiday destinations?

Who, fewer than fifteen years ago, would have predicted that countries like the Czech Republic, Hungary, Poland and Russia itself would emerge from their isolation, participate fully in European trade and become both successful destinations and important generating markets?

Who would have dared foretell that South Africa would achieve intercommunity peace and dialogue, and that it would become Africa's top tourist destination and a source of visitors for its neighbours?

Who would have thought that Greece and Turkey would one day sign an agreement of tourism cooperation and that their tourism sectors would work together for the greater benefit of both countries?

Who would have guessed that western visitors would flock to Cuba in large numbers, to the point where tourism has become the leading sector in the country's economy?

Who, only five years ago, would have believed it possible that tourists from South Korea would go to the North to revisit the places that are dear to them and the relatives they left behind?

Who would have thought that China would allow its citizens to visit as tourists Japan, the Republic of Korea, Australia, New Zealand, the member countries of ASEAN, and now Western Europe? And who can imagine that in less than 15 years from now 100 million Chinese will be visiting other countries, according to our most realistic and conservative forecasts?

Who would have supposed that Israeli visitors would fill the hotels, restaurants and even the casinos of Palestine? This happened only a few years ago in Jericho and Bethlehem. And who would be rash enough to wager that, in spite of the bitter conflicts since, those tourists will not return one day?

At WTO we never fail to stress two clear messages: that tourism can contribute decisively to furthering the peace process between countries. And, that once peace is secured, tourism will be one of the leading economic sectors in each of the countries concerned.

Tourism and peace are inseparable; but they are also very fragile. That lesson we have learned many times since 11 September 2001. Terrorist attacks, the war in Iraq and regional conflicts in many parts of the world constantly remind us that we live in a world full of uncertainties, dangers and new challenges.

Peace is surely the most precious commodity in the world. It represents the first step on the road of development, progress, social order and fulfilment. We need peace to meet the major challenges that threaten our survival: global warming; the erosion of resources such as fresh water and energy that are critical to sustain life on earth; and to be able to deal with the growing problems of malnutrition, disease and poverty.

These challenges were summed up in the United Nations Millennium Declaration of 2000, a commitment to work for a better world which reads: "We are determined to establish a just and lasting peace all over the world."

This Charter identifies several fundamental values, all of which are closely related to the call for Sustainable Tourism that forms the backbone of WTO's Code of Ethics.

They are:

– **Freedom:** Men and women have the right to live their lives and raise their children in dignity, free from hunger and the fear of violence, oppression or injustice.

– **Equality:** No individual and no nation must be denied the opportunity to benefit from development. The equal rights and opportunities of women and men must be assured.

– **Solidarity:** Global challenges must be managed in a way that distributes the cost and burdens fairly in accordance with the basic principles of equity and social justice. Those who suffer or who benefit least deserve help from those who benefit most.

– **Tolerance:** Human beings must respect one another, in all their diversity of belief, culture and language. Differences within and between societies should be neither feared nor repressed, but cherished as a precious asset of humanity. A culture of peace and dialogue among all civilizations should be actively promoted.

– **Respect for Nature:** Prudence must be shown in the management of all living species and natural resources. Only in this way can they be preserved and passed on to our descendants. Current unsustainable patterns of production and consumption must be changed in the interest of our future welfare and that of our descendants, and

– **Shared responsibility:** for managing worldwide economic and social development, as well as threats to international peace and security.

The key to unlock the implementation of the Millennium Declaration is peace. Without a climate of peace we will not succeed in reaching the Goals of the Declaration. There are already indications that we are falling behind schedule. We need peace and a spirit of cooperation to mobilise effectively to achieve these goals.

There is no doubt that tourism can help to strengthen the peace process and promote the fundamental values of the Declaration. Peace and Tourism belong together. Without peace there can be no tourism. But tourism can also contribute to the peace process.

I call peace a process, because it can never be absolute, final or complete. Peace is not a destination, a place where you arrive and unpack. Peace is a journey that demands continued effort. It requires that we vigorously protect and advance those rights and values that form the foundation of real peace. In such a climate tourism will flourish, as will other economic activities.

Tourism is an ally of peace in that it brings people together, teaches them to observe, understand and appreciate the rich diversity of peoples. It creates dialogue between visitor and host, between different cultures, between peoples and places.

Since prehistoric times, travel has served as a means of exploration, trade, pilgrimage, personal enrichment, and encounters between people from different tribes, nations and cultures. But it has also served as a vehicle for territorial expansion, espionage, terrorism, colonialism, slavery, desecration of cultures, exploitation of resources, and war.

Because of these diverse motivations, it is imperative that those of us who work in tourism and long for world peace consider how tourism may be used as a means to build understanding and tolerance between individuals and the nations of this world.

AFRICAN UNION

AFRICAN UNION

Establishment

The advent of the African Union – AU – can be described as an event of great magnitude in the international evolution of the continent.

On 9 September 1999, the Heads of State and Government of the Organization of African Unity issued a Declaration – The Sirte Declaration – calling for the establishment of an African Union, with a view, inter alia, to accelerating the process of integration in the continent to enable it to play its rightful role in the global economy while addressing multifaceted social, economic and political problems compounded as they are by certain negative aspects of globalization.

The African Union was launched in Durban/South Africa at the Durban Summit on 9 July 2002. The Durban Summit convened the First Assembly of the AU Heads of States.

The African Union is headquartered in Addis Ababa, Ethiopia.

The African Union is comprised of 53 Member States.

Executive Head

H. E. Mr. Alpha Oumar Konaré, Chairperson, African Union Commission

Objective

– To achieve greater unity and solidarity between the African countries and the peoples of Africa;

– To defend sovereignty, territorial integrity and independance of its Member States;

– To accelerate the political and socio-economic integration of the continent;

– To promote and defend African common positions on issues of interest to the continent and its peoples;

– To encourage international cooperation, taking due account of the Charter of the United Nations and the Universal Decalaration of Human Rights.

– To promote democratic principles and institutions, popular participation and good governance;

– To promote peace, security, and stability in Africa.

Contact Information

African Union Headquarters

P. O. Box 3243
Addis Ababa
Ethiopia

Telephone: + 251 11 551 77 00
Fax:　　　 + 251 11 551 78 44

Internet:　　**http://www.africa-union.org**

The Emerging African Union Architecture
for Peace and Security in Africa: Challenges and Opportunities

H. E. Mr. Alpha Oumar Konaré, Chairperson of the AU Commission

I. Introduction

Since the birth of the Organization of African Unity (OAU), and more particularly with the collapse of the bi-polar world at the end of the 1990s, the issue of peace, security and stability in Africa has remained a major pre-occupation. The end of the Cold War exposed the critical areas of underachievement in the process of state-building in Africa, which had begun promisingly at the dawn of the 1960s. While the rest of the world was in the throes of a boom arising from the rapid economic and political transformation ushered in by the confluence of globalization and the advancements in science, technology and communication, Africa, on the other hand, suffered from an economic downturn and dwindling economies caused by a number of paralyses. One of such major paralyses was in the realm of peace and security. The continent was inundated by a wave of armed conflicts, coups d'état and political instability of various manifestations, many of which shattered not only the social fabric of societies but also the state institutions and the lifeline of fledging economies in Africa. These developments in a new world economic order that was anchored on globalization and market competition did not bode well for the economies of African States emerging from colonialism.

In order to confront these critical challenges to the continent, it was necessary to make close linkage between the requirements for economic development and the demands for peace and security. More so, was the new awareness that the two complement each other and that a peaceful and secured Africa will guarantee and boost economic development.

It was against this background that African leaders, in their search for more robust and proactive mechanisms to remedy the continent from its paralyses, decided to enter into a new era of greater integration by establishing the African Union, marking a turning point from a politically focused organization to one with focus on economic development. The Constitutive Act of the African Union adopted in Lome in 2001, underscored the fact that the scourge of conflicts in Africa constitutes a major impediment to the socio-economic development of the continent and of the need to promote peace, security and stability as a prerequisite for the implementation of their development and integration agenda. The creation of the African Union was orchestrated by the desire to safe the peoples of Africa from the scourges of conflicts, poverty, underdevelopment, diseases, and the challenges to integration. The main preoccupation of the founders of the Union was the need for economic development but they also understood that this cannot be achieved without peace and security.

The adoption of the Protocol Relating to the Establishment of the Peace and Security Council indicated the determination of African leaders to furnish the new Union with the robust and proactive mechanisms necessary to deal with the daunting challenges of peace and security on the continent. The Protocol itself marked an important evolution in thinking and concern in Africa about the scourge of conflict and the need to eradicate it. It was therefore a practical expression of the need for an operational structure for the promotion and maintenance of peace and security in Africa and for the effective implementation of decisions taken in the areas of conflict prevention, peace-making, peace support operations and rapid intervention as well as to promote the objectives and principles enshrined in the Constitutive Act of the African Union. The key challenges to peace and security in Africa include:

– Armed Conflicts;
– Coups d'Etat and Unconstitutional Changes of Government;
– Peacekeeping and Post-Conflict Peace-Building.

II. Toward a Structured Peace and Security Architecture in Africa: The Cairo Declaration on a Mechanism for Conflict Prevention, Management and Resolution

The OAU's efforts to address the scourge of conflicts in the continent took a turning point in June 1993, when the 29th Ordinary Session of the Assembly of Heads of State and Government, held in Cairo, Egypt, adopted a declaration establishing, within the OAU, a Mechanism for Conflict Prevention, Management and Resolution. The decision to establish the Mechanism was reached against the background of a new awareness on the continent that, there was no way Africa could improve its socio-economic performance in the years following the end of the Cold War in an environment of wars, conflict and political instability. In this respect, it is worth recalling that, three years earlier, in July 1990, the 26th Ordinary Session of the Assembly of Heads of State and Government, that took place in Addis Ababa, adopted the "Declaration on the Political and Socio-Economic Situation in Africa and the Fundamental Changes Taking Place in the World". In that Declaration, the Heads of State and Government noted, that:

"No single internal factor has contributed more to the present socio-economic problems in the Continent than the scourge of conflicts within and between our countries. They have brought about death and human suffering, engendered hate and divided nations and families. Conflicts have forced millions of our people into a drifting life as refugees and internally displaced persons, deprived of their means of livelihood, human dignity and hope. Conflicts have gobbled-up scarce resources, and undermined the ability of our countries to address the many compelling needs of our people."

In the light of many challenges, the Mechanism did not prove all that effective in the preservation of peace and security in the continent. Although it made some achievements, it was faced with serious constraints, which limited its capacity to achieve its mandate. It also encountered many challenges in dealing with conflict situations in Burundi, Comoros, Rwanda, Liberia and others.

III. A New Peace and Security Architecture?

Once the weaknesses of the Mechanism were assessed, it became clear that there was need for a more robust and proactive mechanism, particularly in view of the new political dispensation ushered in by the establishment of the African Union. The new efforts focused on putting in place comprehensive architecture for peace and security, which could address the multifaceted challenges to peace and security in Africa, including peacekeeping. These efforts culminated in the adoption of the Protocol Relating to the Establishment of the Peace and Security Council (PSC) of the African Union.

The PSC, as provided in the Protocol, is to be supported by the African Standby Force (to deal with peace-support operations), the Panel of the Wise, the Continental Early Warning System (CEWS), and the Peace Fund (to garner the necessary resources for the promotion of peace and security). In addition to the PSC Protocol, the peace and security architecture includes, the African Union Non-Aggression and Common Defence Pact, adopted by the 4th Ordinary Session of the Assembly of the Union, held in Abuja, Nigeria, in January 2005; the Common African Defence and Security Policy (CADSP), adopted by the 2nd Extraordinary Session of the Union, held in Sirte, Libya, in February 2005; as well as other security instruments of the Union, such as the Treaty establishing the African Nuclear Weapons Free-zone (the Pelindaba Treaty), and the Convention for the Prevention and Combating of Terrorism. While previous efforts concentrated on conflict resolution, the new peace and security architecture provides for a holistic approach for the promotion of peace and security in Africa.

The adoption of the PSC Protocol and its entrance into force in December 2003, equipped the continent with a more robust apparatus for preserving and enhancing peace and security. The central objectives of the PSC are, among others:

– promote and implement peace-building;
– develop a common defence policy for the Union;
– coordinate and harmonize continental efforts in the prevention and combating of terrorism; and
– promote and encourage democratic practices, good governance and the rule of law, protect human rights and fundamental freedoms.

IV. Making Peacekeeping Work in Africa

The difficulties of the first peacekeeping venture undertaken by the OAU in Chad in 1979 to 1982, coupled with the tragedies in Rwanda and Burundi in the 1990s, provided a new momentum for the need to build the capacity of the continent in the area of peacekeeping.

In order to address these challenges, African Chiefs of Defence Staff (ACDS) met in Addis Ababa, from 3 to 6 June 1996, emphasized that the primary responsibility of the OAU should lie with the anticipation and prevention of conflicts, in accordance with the relevant provisions of the 1993 Cairo Declaration. They also recognized that the primary responsibility for the maintenance of international peace and security, particularly in the area of peacekeeping, rests with the United Nations Security

Council. At the same time, the meeting recognized that certain exceptional circumstances can arise which may lead to the deployment of limited peacekeeping or observation missions by the OAU. Subsequently, as reflected below, the 2nd ACDS meeting took place in Harare, from 20 to 22 October 1997, to further the work initiated by the first meeting. And long after, the third meeting of the ACDS, and including the participation of governmental experts from AU member States, took place in Addis Ababa, from 15 to 16 May 2003. Notably, the third meeting came in the work of the decision taken by the Assembly of the Union at its Maputo Summit, held in July 2003, relating to the operationalisation of the Peace and Security Council of the African Union.

The 2nd ACDS Meeting in Harare, from 24 to 25 October 1997, convened to consider the recommendations, observations and proposals of the Group of Military Experts, discussed among others:

– The concept of peace support operations (PSO);
– Applicable procedures and adequacy of structures for PSO;
– Command and control of OAU PSO at various levels;
– Command and control of joint OAU/UN and OAU/Regional Organization
  operations;
– Planning and structure of PSO communications;
– Capacity building of Africa and the OAU General secretariat in the field of PSO;
– Logistic support and financing of OAU PSO.

However, even in the best of circumstances where the UN fully assumes its responsibilities on the Continent, the OAU had no option but to develop its civilian and military missions of observation and monitoring of limited scope and duration. There is therefore the need to revisit the earlier decision of the OAU for the establishment of the 500-man standby observer force. The rationale for this proposition was that:

– there are low intensity conflicts in which the UN will not be involved, as they can
  be dealt with by the Regional Organisation, such as the Comoros;
– even in the case of conflicts where the UN has decided to deploy a peacekeeping
  mission, the procurement and logistical requirements are such that there is a long
  delay before the mission becomes operational. Pending that actual deployment of
  the UN mission, there can be the need for a provisional deployment, in order to
  ensure that the peace process is not derailed. A classic example of this situation was

the deployment of the OAU Neutral Investigators in the DRC in 1999–2000 prior to the deployment of MONUC, and the deployment of the African Mission in Burundi (AMIB) before the deployment of the UN Mission some months later;

– in some conflict situations in which the OAU had played a lead political role, and in which the UN has subsequently assumed the responsibility for the deployment of a peacekeeping mission, there can still be the need for the OAU to maintain a peacekeeping role in the peace process by co-deploying an OAU mission, such as in the Ethiopia-Eritrea peace process;

– the OAU should take into account the new developments arising from the recommendations of the Brahimi Panel, which was convened in 2000 to "assess the shortcomings of the existing system and make frank, specific and realistic recommendations for change." While, on the one hand the recommendations generally offer opportunities for closer UN-OAU co-operation, they also fundamentally affect the ability of the OAU and its Member States to fully and effectively participate in the UN Standby Arrangements System (UNSAS), and peacekeeping in general.

V. Non-Interference Doesn't Mean Indifference

Since this idea of non-interference and responsiveness was first mooted without any in-depth conceptualization apart from identifying areas where there can be potential contentions and as a result demanding the need for some form of response from the African Union, this section of the paper will endeavour to tease out what the main outlines of this proactive and assertive policy is.

In its original conceptualization, security as understood by the African Union went beyond the ramification of the state to involve human security. Due to the complexity of challenges faced by the African continent and the old notion of non-intervention in the internal affairs of member states, the problems faced by states is contributing to the idea that:

> "The notion of non-interference must be revised because it must be
> never associated with indifference. And this non-indifference must
> lead to coercive measures, to well-adapted and active policies'."[2]

In whatever sense one examines this statement, this is a radical departure from the nature of traditional African international relations as has developed since 1963.

Although in the Constitutive Act of the African Union the principles and norms that underpin the union are enunciated, it is important that what this paper perceives as a radical conceptual shift described above must be situated within what the Act posits.[3] It is important to appreciate the context within which the African Union is developing specific "principles" to guide community action. What can be deduced is that by emphasizing of issues of security (among a panoply of other issue-areas), the African Union is developing into a regime with specific rules and principles. Rules in this sense "… relate to the written rules and guidelines within the specific issue area that the signatory states essentially have voluntarily accepted to uphold". Furthermore, and in the same vein, "principles are the results of the development of a common understanding and collective interpretation of reality of individual incidents … that affect member states". To that end, several questions arise of which they will need to be disaggregated and examined. First, what explains this radical shift in approach and methodology? Secondly, what is the level of bindingness; understood as the level of political willingness of structural commitments that member states have made to employ such coercive measures? What role, if any, have epistemic communities played in bringing about this critical change in policy?

Finally, what set of occurrences will elicit such responses which demonstrate the characterization of the African Union as "exist(ing) and keep(ing) its promises of rebirth" which are issues of security, defence and economic development?

A series of incidents are identified as potentially warranting coercive measures:

– The first identifiable incident deals with cases where there has
  been constitutional illegalities or changes of government;[6]
– The demarcation of boundaries; and
– The issue of the fairness of elections.[7]

The above, therefore, is the extent to which the idea of non-intervention but responsiveness should be seen. Although the concept, as has been enunciated, will be challenging in praxis it is not impossible to implement. However, what is critical in this discussion is the political will to apply coercive measures when it becomes imperative. Not only that, there might arise a situation where there is the need to disaggregate the type of coercive measures that are anticipated in terms of state size. Although this issue has not yet arisen, it is critical that there is thinking about how best to respond to any challenge that arises from having to respond coercively to a large state.

VI. The African Standby Force and the Future of Peacekeeping in Africa

The Constitutive Act, particularly, its Article 4(h) which provides for the right of the Union to intervene in a Member State pursuant to a decision of the Assembly in respect of grave circumstances, namely: war crimes, genocide and crimes against humanity; clears the way for rapid deployment of peace-support operations in Africa by removing the historic roadblock to collective security on the continent – the principle of non-interference in the internal matters of Member State. One of the fundamental principles of the African Union today is that interference is not non-indifference. The PSC Protocol was built on this new paradigm of collective security in Africa, which inspired the conceptualization of the ASF in its Article 13.

The raison d'être for the establishment of the African Standby Force (ASF) was to endow the PSC with a sound mechanism for rapid deployment of peace support missions. As implicit in its name, the ASF is based on the concept of Standby or "ready to go" arrangement. The Protocol provides that such Force or arrangement be composed of standby multidisciplinary contingents, with civilian and military components based in Member States. The ASF is mandated to take action in the following areas:

– Observation and monitoring missions;
– Other types of peace support operations;
– Intervention in a Member State with respect to grave circumstances or at the request of a Member State in order to restore peace and stability in consonance with Article 4(h) of the Constitutive Act;
– Preventive deployment (to prevent crises before they escalate);
– Peace-building, including post-conflict reconstruction, disarmament, and demobilization;
– Humanitarian assistance and any other functions mandated to it by the PSC.

The ASF is based on the concept of regional brigades. Each of the five regions in Africa is to establish a brigade, which can be deployed at any time. The legitimate mandating authority for the deployment of a brigade is the Peace and Security Council of the AU, in conformity with Chapter VIII of the UN Charter. This means the command Headquarters shall be at the Headquarters of the African Union.

VII. ASF Deployment Missions' Scenarios

Six main scenarios have been envisaged for the deployment of the ASF:

A. Scenario 1:

AU and Regional Organization Military advice to a political mission;

B. Scenario 2:

AU and Regional Organization Military Observer mission co-deployed with the UN mission;

C. Scenario 3:

Standalone AU and Regional Organization observer mission;

D. Scenario 4:

AU and Regional Organization peacekeeping force for Chapter VI of the UN Charter and preventive deployment missions;

E. Scenario 5:

AU peacekeeping for complex multidimensional peacekeeping mission – low level spoilers (as in many of the ongoing conflicts);

F. Scenario 6:

AU intervention, e. g. in the case of genocide, or where the international community does not act promptly.

Each scenario shall be determined by the situation on the ground. The decision on which brigade to deploy shall also be guided by analysis of the crisis and the best scenario.

VIII. Conclusion

While the peace and security agenda set out in the overall AU framework, including the NEPAD programme reflects the collective aspiration of Africans, the AU leadership is keenly aware that these objectives cannot be realized in the short term. A number of potential challenges must be addressed in the short to medium term.

First, it is envisaged that the ASF will respond to diverse operational environments varying from situations requiring preventive deployment to enforcement operations. Therefore, an African Stand-by Force will require careful strategic planning and incremental build up from national to sub-regional levels.

Second, the development of a common doctrine will be particularly challenging. Much will depend on the nature of the operational environment and development of a common concept of operations, at least at sub-regional levels. This is compounded by the fact that the operational environment in which the ASF will operate is not stagnant. As more civil wars are resolved, the nature of the threat emerging from the national level will change, possibly resulting in a return to a murkier operational environment dominated by low-intensity conflicts generated by intra and inter-communal conflicts.

As part of the effort to overcome some of these challenges, it may be more rewarding to create a division of labour, in various aspects of peace support operations, particularly among Member States with a tradition of contributing to peace missions. This might provide a first level of preparation toward the creation of a Stand-by Force. Experiences acquired from participation in African peace operations have shown (even if informally) that certain countries have particular skills and a higher level of preparedness in specific aspects of peace support operations. For example, it is assumed that the Nigerian and Guinean armed forces are more effective as a crack force for peace enforcement while the Ghanaian army is believed to be more experienced in traditional peacekeeping.

Specialization and training should cover activities along a spectrum – from peacekeeping to reconstruction, including preventive deployment, peacekeeping, enforcement operations, disarming of armed groups, training of military and police personnel and assistance toward overall institutional reform and provision of logistical support through these phases. Training should also be targeted at Member States that not only have the capacity to contribute troops to peace operations, but that have a track record of contributing to peace operations and can make them available when the need arises.

Not least, and perhaps a central pillar of the whole African philosophy of preserving peace and security in the continent, is the need to enhance per capita freedom, democratic space, enjoyment of human rights and protection, and access to the opportunities for self-development throughout the continent. These aspects should be promoted around each individual, with the progress being measured at each individual level. The conflicts ravaging the continent and its people and their economies are directly linked to deep-seated deprivations that the populations live on a daily basis. Now, there being no fairly large enough space for the affected populations to address those deprivations in a peaceful manner in most cases, protracted violent conflicts become inevitable. The net result is the resort to more expensive methods of managing and resolving those conflicts, whereby enormous quantities of human, financial, logistical and technical resources, otherwise to be devoted to real socio-economic development, are absorbed into operations to restore peace and security.

1   This idea was first mooted in Konare, Alpha Oumar. 2004. "Security is the African Union's priority", African Geopolitics, No. 13, Winter 2004 at http://www.african-geopolitics.org/show.aspx?articleid=3669 accessed on 8 March 2004

2   ibid, p. 2 Our emphasis

3   See especially the Constitutive Act of the African Union, Articles 4(g) which states that "The Union shall function in accordance with the following principles non-interference by any Member State in the internal affairs of another"; and 4(h) the right of the Union to intervene in a Member State pursuant to a decision of the Assembly in respect of grave circumstances, namely: war crimes, genocide and crimes against humanity

4   For further exposition, see Aning, K. 1998 Security in the West African Sub-region: An Analysis of ECOWAS's Policies in Liberia.(Copenhagen: Reprocentre) pp. 48ff

5   ibid, p. 1

6   See Decisions AHG/Dec.141 (XXXV) and AHG/Dec.142 (XXXV) on Unconstitutional Changes of Government adopted by the 35 Ordinary Session of the Assembly of Heads of State and Government of the OAU held in Algiers, Algeria from 12–14 July 1999, and Declaration AHG/Decl.5 (XXXVI) on the Framework for an OAU Response to Unconstitutional Changes of Government, adopted by the 36 Ordinary Session of the Assembly of Heads of State and Government of the OAU, held in Lome, Togo from 10–12 July 2000

7   Konare, op cit, p. 3

ANDEAN COMMUNITY

ANDEAN COMMUNITY

Establishment

The early beginnings of the Andean Community date back to 1969, when a group of South American countries signed the Cartagena Agreement, also known as the Andean Pact, for the purpose of establishing a customs union within a period of ten years.

Over the next three decades, Andean integration passed though a series of different stages.

A basically closed conception of inward-looking integration based on the import substitution model gradually gave way to a scheme of open regionalism.

The progress of integration and the emergence of new challenges stemming from global economic change brought to the fore the need for both institutional and policy reforms in the Cartagena Agreement. These were accomplished through the Protocols of Trujillo and Sucre, respectively. The institutional reforms gave the process political direction and created the Andean Community and the Andean Integration System. The policy reforms, for their part, extended the scope of integration beyond the purely trade and economic areas.

The Andean Community started operating on August 1, 1997 with a General Secretariat, whose headquarters are in Lima, Peru, as its executive body.

The Andean Community is a subregional organization endowed with an international legal status, which is made up of Bolivia, Colombia, Ecuador, Peru and Venezuela and the bodies and institutions comprising the Andean Integration System – AIS – .

Located in South America, the five Andean countries together have 120 million inhabitants living in an area of 4 700 000 square kilometers.

Executive Head

H. E. Mr. Allan Wagner Tizón, Secretary-General of the Andean Community

Objectives

The key objectives of the Andean Community are: to promote the balanced and harmonious development of the member countries under equitable conditions, to boost their growth through integration and economic and social cooperation, to enhance participation in the regional integration process with a view to the progressive formation of a Latin American common market, and to strive for steady improvement in the standard of living of their inhabitants.

Contact Information

Andean Community

General Secretariat
Paseo de la República 3895
Esq. Aramburú, San Isidro
Lima 27
Peru

Telephone: + 511 411 14 00
Fax: + 511 221 33 29

Internet: **http://www.comunidadandina.org**

Andean Community Contributions to Peace and Security in a Multilateral World

H. E. Mr. Allan Wagner Tizón, Secretary-General of the Andean Community

Introduction

The end purpose of the Andean integration process – the Cartagena Agreement –, known today as the Andean Community,[1] has been, from its very origin at the close of the sixties, the continuous improvement of living standards among the subregion's inhabitants as a result of the balanced and harmonious development of the Member Countries under equitable conditions, due to integration and economic and social cooperation.[2]

As a result, Andean integration and cooperation are grounded in principles of equality, justice, peace, solidarity and democracy that are also essential for comprehensive development and the strengthening of multilateral relations in a context of globalization.

It is a fact that globalization offers our societies vast opportunities to increase their trade presence. But in altering the dynamics of international relations – by generating knowledge and applied technologies, incorporating new actors, organizing transnational networks and reducing transaction costs, among other things – it has contributed to growing interdependence among States as a means of coping effectively with the challenges created by those changes at both the local and international levels.

In this context, the equitable distribution of the benefits of worldwide economic growth and of its consequent transformation into integral global, regional and local development policies and strategies and the incorporation of the less favored population sectors with a view to progressively overcome historical economic and social gaps, has assumed special importance.

This latter aim is, without a doubt, a basic pillar of the new conception of security and of its undeniable links with the integral development of contemporary societies.

An Andean vision

Security, from an Andean viewpoint, is a situation in which State and society are protected from threats or risks that could jeopardize integral development and the well being of citizens, as well as the unhampered exercise of their rights and freedoms in an environment of fully effective democracy.[3]

Its nature, as a result, is multidimensional and comprehensive, covering political, economic, social and cultural issues, and is reflected in policies in spheres as varied as the strengthening of democratic institutions and the State of Law, defense, health, the environment, economic development and the prevention of natural disasters, among others.

In this connection, it should be stressed that security is a public good, which the State, as the sole actor authorized to exercise a monopoly over the legitimate use of force, should guarantee, irrespective of the shared responsibility of all public and private actors and agents for its progressive reinforcement and consolidation.

Furthermore, by making man the main subject of the initiatives and actions undertaken in this area, the new vision goes beyond the traditional view of State protection as territorial defense, in which other States are necessarily identified as the threat.

This change is also consistent with the adoption of new approaches toward distinguishing peace zones, instruments the United Nations has been using since the seventies to remove specific geographic areas – the Indian Ocean (1971) and the South Atlantic (1986) – from the sphere of geostrategic confrontation and the so-called "nuclear race" among the major powers.

The post-Cold War international security agenda has, in point of fact, allowed the nature and scope of this concept to evolve. While keeping prohibition of the use of weapons of mass destruction as its core element, the notion of the peace zone has been enriched by the definition of a frame of reference for internal action, cooperation and peaceful dispute settlement among the States involved.

Therefore, it means establishing relations of trust and complementarity, arranging for cooperative actions to confront common threats and sending a signal of stability to the international community aimed at reinforcing respect for the integrity, sovereignty, and self-determination of the States comprising the peace zone.

Concrete Developments

The "Declaration regarding a South American Peace Zone" adopted by the South American Presidents at their Second Meeting, in Guayaquil, Ecuador, on July 26 and 27, 2002, based on the "Lima Commitment: Andean Charter for Peace and Security and the Limitation and Control of the Expenditure on Foreign Defense," signed on June 17, 2002, together with the corresponding initiatives of the Southern Common Market, reflect the conviction shared throughout the entire region that the nations' development and integral well-being should rest on foundations of peace, security and cooperation.

The "Declaration of San Francisco de Quito on the Establishment and Development of an Andean Peace Zone" adopted during the Fifteenth Andean Presidential Council on July 12, 2004, further enhances the scope of the South American Peace Zone and defines its characteristic geographic area, foundations, elements and objectives, in keeping with the Andean democratic, cooperative and non-offensive conception of security.

It also envisages the guidelines for its consolidation and international projection, with a view toward contributing to the development of the South American Peace Zone, the strengthening of world peace and the construction of a more balanced and representative international order, among other things.

Its key objectives include boosting the development and reinforcement of democratic values, principles and practices and, among them, the political and institutional systems of the Member Countries and of the region as a whole, with justice, cohesion and social equity.

As a result, the Andean Peace Zone aims primarily to develop the necessary conditions for the peaceful and concerted resolution of conflicts, whatever their nature, and of their causes, without denying the importance, in the present international context, of ensuring the effective prohibition of weapons of mass destruction – nuclear, chemical, biological and toxic, – including their movement through the subregion.

The Member Countries are accordingly invited to define a general framework of principles and options that will allow the parties to a dispute that is not subject to the jurisdiction of bodies belonging to the Andean Integration System, to reach a settlement.

It further points out that teaching a culture of peace and integration is an essential requirement for strengthening peaceful coexistence, an identity and a feeling of belonging among Andean Community citizens – elements that are inherent to the deepening of Andean integration and that are incorporated in the new Strategic Design for the Subregional integration process.

By the same token, it should also contribute to the thorough implementation of the "Guidelines of an Andean Common External Security Policy," adopted through Decision 587 of the Andean Council of Foreign Ministers during the above-cited Presidential Summit, and their merging with other Community policies and undertakings in the spheres of Social Development, Environmental and Biodiversity Management and human rights.

It should be noted that both instruments were the result of a wide-ranging process of consultations with public and private actors and agents from the most varying sectors of our societies, a process that not only legitimates their objectives and scopes, but also seeks to encourage reflection on the restructuring of relations between the State, its institutions and its citizens, in strategic areas.

Another significant advance in Andean Common Foreign Policy, Decision 587, substantiates and complements the commitments and actions that will make it possible to create the necessary conditions for achieving lasting peace and stability in the subregion from the outlook of cooperation on and harmonization of security policy.

In point of fact, this policy appears in the initial analysis to be a peace option. Its main purpose is to prevent and combat threats to security in a cooperative and coordinated way, regardless of their nature, within a democratic and non-offensive conception of external security, while promoting the necessary conditions to give the people free and equal access to an environment that is conducive to their material and spiritual fulfillment.

The institutional mechanisms established in the above-cited Lima Commitment are consolidated and deepened in order to accomplish this by incorporating into the dialogue and harmonization process, other actors competent in security matters, together with broad sectors of civil society. Security is reaffirmed as being the task of society as a whole, without overlooking the State's basic responsibility, meaning that confidence levels must be raised in the subregion in order to achieve the planned objectives.

As a result, the first specific mandate handed down by that binding legal instrument is to design an Andean Program of Confidence and Security-Building Measures based on the advances made by Member Countries in their relations with neighboring countries, in the Lima Commitment and in the agreements reached within the Organization of American States, particularly the Declarations of Santiago (1995) and of San Salvador (1998) and the Consensus of Miami (February 2003).

In concluding, attention should be drawn to United Nations General Assembly Resolution 59/54 of December 2, 2004, welcoming with satisfaction the Declaration of the Andean Zone of Peace and recognizing its contribution toward strengthening international peace and security.

Prospects

The significant regulatory advances made by the Andean Community with regard to peace and security should be viewed as the start of a broad-ranging process whose success will depend largely on the sustained political will of our societies to work toward building a common area of peace, internal security and justice.

This will require appropriating agreements reached by public and private actors and agents in the Member Countries that are essential for guaranteeing the necessary legitimacy and sustainability of Community policies and strategies. These should be reflected in national and even local actions, at the same time as local initiatives adopted in response to specific security problems are projected toward the subregional and world arenas. This process should contribute initially towards strengthening democratic governance, promoting stability in the subregion and, finally, encouraging a fuller presence in and influence on decision-making to build a collective and cooperative security system.

It is evident that the success of actions undertaken within the framework of these Community policies can be evaluated, solely and exclusively, in terms of the degree to which cooperation at the operative level is able to build up the capacity of the countries and of the subregion to respond effectively to the threats, particularly the so-called "new threats" that are transnational in nature and, in most cases, "non-State" in origin.

It will also depend upon the capacity of the Andean Community to implement the items provided for in the Andean Common External Security Policy agenda with flexibility, coherently and progressively. The mere fact of moving ahead with the dialogue and harmonizing of priorities is, in itself, an accomplishment, given the sensitive nature of the issues involved and each Member Country's varying perception of the risks of the different threats, and these advances will encourage the exchange of knowledge and experiences and the quantifying of resources available to confront threats jointly.

From this outlook, it is not a question of merely combining national strategies to prevent and combat threats or elements of risk, but of an interlinked and conscious effort to evaluate the causes, mechanisms and processes that facilitate their proliferation. In this sense, it represents a substantial contribution by the Andean Subregion to the international community toward overcoming these threats in a cooperative and coordinated way.

This, in turn, would mean actually making the necessary institutional reforms in our societies that would allow for the materialization of the shared responsibility at all levels for consolidating security – in other words, reshaping civil-military relations so that traditional biases in attributing power to national authorities are set aside and more transparency is attained in public management.

To conclude, the Andean Subregion and the international community should take advantage of the unprecedented opportunity to revert the trends that have made it possible to define international security relations in terms of zero sum games, by designing and implementing a cooperative security system that would produce scenarios in which we could all emerge triumphant in effectively confronting threats, worries and other challenges for the benefit of our nations' integral development.

---

1   The Andean Community is a subregional organization with an international legal status, of which Bolivia, Colombia, Ecuador, Peru and Venezuela are Members and which is made up of the bodies and institutions of the Andean Integration System (AIS).

2   Article 1 of the Andean Subregional Integration Agreement – the Cartagena Agreement.

3   First Meeting of the High-Level Group on Security and Confidence-Building, Bogotá, February 28, 2003. Countersigned by the Andean Council of Foreign Ministers

ASIA-EUROPE FOUNDATION

ASIA-EUROPE FOUNDATION

Establishment

The Asia-Europe Foundation (ASEF) was established in February 1997 by the members of the Asia-Europe Meeting (ASEM). ASEF is based in Singapore and reports to a board of 39 governors representing the 38 ASEM countries and the European Commission.

The ASEM/ASEF member countries are:
Austria, Belgium, Brunei, Cambodia, China, Cyprus, Czech Republic, Denmark, Estonia, Finland, France, Germany, Greece, Hungary, Indonesia, Ireland, Italy, Japan, Laos, Latvia, Lithuania, Luxembourg, Malaysia, Malta, Myanmar, Netherlands, Philippines, Poland, Portugal, Singapore, Slovakia, Slovenia, South Korea, Spain, Sweden, Thailand, United Kingdom and Vietnam.

The Asia-Europe Foundation is funded by contributions from the member governments, but the cost of many of its projects are shared by other institutions as well as private corporations of ASEM countries.

Executive Head

H. E. Mr. Cho Won-il, Executive Director of the Asia-Europe Foundation

Objectives

The Asia-Europe Foundation seeks to promote better mutual understanding between the peoples of Asia and Europe through greater intellectual, cultural, and people-to-people exchanges.

One way ASEF carries out its mandate is by creating its own projects. Some of these initiatives include Asia-Europe Lecture, Asia-Europe Young Artists' Painting Competition and Exhibition, Informal Human Rights Seminar, Asia-Europe Youth Co-operation Network, and ASEF Editors' Roundtable.

Having completed over 350 projects directly involving 17,000 people to date, ASEF always seeks to work in partnership with other institutions and private sector entities to ensure its work is broad-based and spread as widely as possible throughout ASEM member countries.

Contact Information

Asia-Europe Foundation

31 Heng Mui Keng Terrace
Singapore 119595

Telephone: + 65 68 74 97 00
Fax: + 65 68 72 12 06

Internet: **http://www.asef.org**

The Work and Mission of the Asia-Europe Foundation

H. E. Mr. Cho Won-il, Executive Director

The world heaved a sigh of relief at the end of the Cold War. With the conclusion of this chapter of world history, conflicts and tension inherent in the bipolar world system were given new avenues to reach their resolutions. We anticipated a new era of peace and international stability. Surely, the stride of scientific and technological advancements in conjunction with an universal free-market capitalism would march us towards an interconnected and interdependent global village. Yet, instability, security challenges and international conflicts together with underdevelopment, poverty, starvation, lack of democracy, disrespect for human rights are still not far from our mind. In the past decade, the world has changed faster and more profoundly. Issues that reek of traditional tension and conflicts are now compounded with new complications.

Today, one can see that the global leaders and community are grappling with the swiftness at which international situations unfold and are struggling to devise new responses for contemporary international conflicts and issues. The shape of international affairs now and in the future depends on the definition of long-term economic, technological, military and socio-political policies. A harmonized international system with a new balance of power and new structures must eventually be adopted.

As Longin Pastusiak[1] has suggested, "The new world order also means a higher role for diplomacy and diplomatic techniques of international conflict resolution. It means shifting the emphasis from military to diplomatic methods." And diplomacy should, basically, rely on dialogue and mutual understanding.

Indeed, with the advent of globalisation, the need to facilitate and promote dialogue and, therefore, greater understanding among cultures and people is even greater. We need no introduction to examples where the lack of understanding and awareness can snowball into disastrous and violent consequences. To foster meaningful dialogue, which is critical for mutual understanding, we need new and innovative instruments.

The Asia-Europe Foundation (ASEF) is one unique instrument created by the members of the Asia-Europe Meeting (ASEM) to meet the challenges of this new world order.

Apart from the two traditional pillars of international relations – political and econo-mic, ASEF is erected as a third pillar of Asia-Europe cooperation. Formed with the purpose of strengthening the links between civil societies of Asia and Europe, ASEF seeks to promote better mutual understanding between the peoples of Asia and Europe through greater intellectual, cultural and people-to-people exchanges between the two regions. The founding spirit of ASEF is based on the belief that constant interaction and dialogues are pre-requisites for understanding and respecting the wide range of differences in customs, heritages, values and behaviour.

For this purpose, and to allow flexibility and most appropriate responses to the needs of civil society, ASEF was established as a not-for-profit foundation instead of an inter-governmental agency. This indeed provided ASEF a higher capacity to deal with other institutions of civil societies such as universities, NGOs and other foun-dations. Together, the member countries represent 40 % of the world's population, 50 % of its GNP, and 55 % of global trade. Thirty-eight sovereign countries[2] and the European Commission jointly pledged to fund this foundation, which is actually tan-tamount to a kind of privatization of a function that had hitherto been the territory of States. This is a first in the history of international organisations.

To date, ASEF has completed over 350 projects involving more than 17,000 Asians and Europeans in the past eight years of promoting dialogue among civilisations. ASEF's activities are diverse in nature. Furthermore, to ensure that ASEF's work has a broad base and a multilateral outreach throughout ASEM member countries, we always seek to work in partnership with other institutions and private sector entities.

Structure of ASEF

Mr. Renaud Donnedieu De Vabres, French Minister of Culture and Communications, noted at the opening address for the second ASEM Culture Ministers' Meeting, "ASEM possess a formidable tool for implementing (multilateral initiatives) in the shape of the Asia-Europe Foundation (ASEF), based in Singapore. I want to stress here the fundamental role ASEF is playing in the practical and effective promotion of dialogue among civilisations."

Structurally, ASEF is organised into four portfolios and is managed by an executive director, Ambassador Cho Won-il and his deputy, Mr. Hendrik Kloninger. The decision-making body of ASEF is the Board of Governors, comprising 39 high-profile individuals nominated by member governments. Led currently by Ambassador Paul R. Brouwer (The Netherlands), the Board of The Directorate of Intellectual Exchange, led by Bertrand Fort, aims to contribute to policy and academic debates as well as strategic thinking on common themes of current and future multilateral importance between Asia and Europe, playing the role of a think-tank for the policymakers of the Asia-Europe Meeting. Intellectual Exchange's programme areas include – international relations; governance; education, science, and technology; and, cultures and civilisations dialogue. Participants of such programmes are drawn from academia, the media, government or private institutions, research centres, think-tanks, non-government organisations (NGOs), trade unions, foundations, "Asian Houses" in Europe, "European Houses" in Asia, private establishments and others.

Since 1998, the Intellectual Exchange Department has provided the institutional backbone of ASEM's political process for its human rights dialogue, and has embarked on gender issues, justice, labour relations, religious and interfaith dialogue. The objective is to engender ground-breaking initiatives and recommendations for government-civil society dialogue parallel to ASEM's priorities. During their meetings, network links are created with the aim of increasing awareness of the issues and cooperative initiatives. A good example is the Asia-Europe Environmental Forum, the only civil society platform of dialogue and cooperation between civil societies of the two regions.

The People-to-People Exchange Department, managed by Ramon Molina, works to foster dialogue and forge networks among the next generation of leaders and decision-makers. Special emphasis is given to the younger generation, in line with the importance attached by the ASEM leaders to the role of the youth and young people in strengthening the foundation of the Asia-Europe partnership. Consistent with this strategic orientation, P2P has developed three main streams of activities. The first stream comprises activities to strengthen inter-regional contacts and exchanges in the field of education. The second stream consists of activities that are targeted at enhancing dialogue and co-operation among the youth of Asia and Europe. The third and final stream is made up of activities to provide regular platforms for young leaders in different sectors of the two regions to meet and discuss issues of mutual interest.

Programmes such as the biannual ASEF University, a two-week academic enrichment programme for outstanding undergraduates in Asia and Europe, are designed to encourage intercultural exchange among students from the two regions. As testament of the effectiveness of this programme, the ASEF University Alumni Network, an independent association, was erected by participants of previous ASEF University programme sessions to build on their interest in Asia-Europe issues and to contribute to promoting people-to-people links and intellectual exchanges among students and young people.

His Royal Highness Prince Haji Al-Muhtadee Billah, the Crown Prince and Senior Minister at the Prime Minister's Office of Brunei attested to the importance of this programme in a newspaper interview – "By promoting better understanding between our two regions, through a process of dialogue, personal interaction and collaborative learning, the ASEF programme creates opportunities for young people to work together to envision a common future and to solve common problems."

Chulamanee Chartsuwan is at the helm of the Cultural Exchange directorate. This department aims to promote exchanges on certain process in cultural and artistic fields. The main areas include: young artists' exchanges, process-oriented platforms for exchange, dialogue on cultural policy, as well as spearheading a process towards the development of a multi-disciplinary cultural portal for Asia and Europe.

The department runs various long-term programmes and activities. Young artists benefit greatly from the young artist exchange programmes. AS Louise Furh from Denmark commented after her participation in the Asia-Europe Art Camp held in Tokyo in November 2004, "I am very glad to have participated and very grateful for the concern from people like you. ASEF has given possibilities for artists to meet, exchange and develop ideas, which I think is very useful and important."

In the field of cinema, young film professionals are supported through the Cultural Exchange's film development plan meetings, cultural grants and an online portal for film practitioners – http://sea-images.asef.org. A programme that works to facilitate the sharing of our joint Euro-Asian cultural heritage is the Asia-Europe Museum Network (ASEMUS), which was set up in 2001. ASEMUS aims to develop mechanisms and projects to redress the asymmetry in museum collections, to pool resources and jointly use the collections to develop professional expertise, and to produce new types of joint, innovative exhibitions and public programmes.

Chin Hock Seng leads the Public Affairs Department. The department endeavours to promote the profile of ASEF as well as raise general awareness of issues pertaining to cross-continental relations by working through the media and other mass-communication channels. Projects such as the Asia-Europe TV Documentary Series, Editors' Roundtables and Journalists' Seminars have brought together media practitioners and other influential and prominent figures to discuss topics ranging from headline-making events to media practices. In each activity, emphasis is placed on multilateral approaches and the importance of cross-cultural understanding. The department also publishes the organisation's Annual Report, the ASEF Newsletters, and on a more academic level, the Asia-Europe Journal, a refereed quarterly journal devoted to intercultural studies in the social sciences and humanities.

Conclusion

The forces of globalisation can bring the world together or tear it apart. For a sustainable future, world stability and the shaping of a culture of peace must be a long-term goal in every countries' agenda. The Deputy Head of the Delegation of the European Commission to Japan, Dr. Michael Reiterer has noted that "ASEF is tasked to fulfil a specific function in the bi-regional context, fitting well into the overall context of the preservation of international peace." Asia and Europe make up a substantial part of the world. The international community as a whole will profit from the sensitization and the subsequent cooperation and dialogue among the world's oldest civilisations.

1   Since October 2001, Longin Pastusiak is the speaker of the Senate of Poland as well as the chair of Poland's permanent delegation to NATO Parliamentary Assembly.

2   ASEM/ASEF members are: Austria, Belgium, Brunei, Cambodia, China, Cyprus, Czech Republic, Denmark, Estonia, Finland, France, Germany, Greece, Hungary, Indonesia, Ireland, Italy, Japan, Laos, Latvia, Lithuania, Luxembourg, Malaysia, Malta, Myanmar, Netherlands, Philippines, Poland, Portugal, Singapore, Slovakia, Slovenia, South Korea, Spain, Sweden, Thailand, United Kingdom and Vietnam

ASSOCIATION OF CARIBBEAN STATES

ASSOCIATION OF CARIBBEAN STATES

Establishment

The Convention Establishing the Association of Caribbean States (ACS) was signed on 24 July 1994 in Cartagena de Indias, Colombia, with the aim of promoting consultation, cooperation and concerted action among all the countries of the Caribbean, comprising 25 Member States and three Associate Members. Eight other non-independent Caribbean countries are eligible for associate membership.

The ACS Member States are:
Antigua and Barbuda, Bahamas, Barbados, Belize, Colombia, Costa Rica, Cuba, Dominica, Dominican Republic, El Salvador, Grenada, Guatemala, Guyana, Haiti, Honduras, Jamaica, Mexico, Nicaragua, Panama, Saint Kitts and Nevis, Saint Lucia, Saint Vincent and the Grenadines, Suriname, Trinidad and Tobago, Venezuela.

The ACS Associate Member States are:
Aruba, France (on behalf of French Guiana, Guadeloupe and Martinique) and the Netherlands Antilles.

The Association of Caribbean States is headquartered in Port of Spain, Trinidad and Tobago.

Executive Head

H. E. Dr. Rubén Arturo Silié Valdez, Secretary-General of ACS

Objectives

The objectives of the Association of Caribbean States are enshrined in the Convention and are based on the following:

– the strengthening of the regional co-operation and integration process, with a view to creating an enhanced economic space in the region;

– preserving the environmental integrity of the Caribbean Sea which is regarded as the common patrimony of the peoples of the region; and

– and promoting the sustainable development of the Greater Caribbean.

The Greater Caribbean Zone of Co-operation was established in recognition of the common geographic space shared by the ACS Member States, Countries and Territories, and the common interests and objectives derived therefrom. The Greater Caribbean Zone of Co-operation consists of joint actions in the priority areas of the ACS, namely, Trade, Sustainable Tourism, Transport and Natural Disasters.

Contact Information

Association of Caribbean States

5-7 Sweet Briar Road, Saint Clair
P. O. Box 660
Port of Spain, Trinidad and Tobago
West Indies

Telephone: + 1 868 622 9575
Fax: + 1 868 622 1653

Internet: **http://www.acs-aec.org**

Building a Culture of Peace in the Greater Caribbean

H. E. Dr. Rubén Silié Valdez, Secretary-General of ACS
and Taryn Lesser

Origins and Agenda

Facing the threat of economic marginalization caused by the globalisation of the world economy and increased trade liberalization, in 1993 the Caribbean Community (CARICOM) set up the West Indian Commission that proposed the formation of the Association of Caribbean States (ACS or the "Association"). The convention to establish the organisation was signed shortly thereafter in July 1994.[1] The primary goal of the Association was to integrate all countries and small island nations bordering the Caribbean Sea[2] – and the addition of three Associate Members (Aruba, the Netherlands Antilles, and France on behalf of French Guiana, Guadeloupe and Martinique) – in order to increase cooperation in the trade, tourism and transportation sectors among the English, Spanish and French-speaking states that comprise the "Greater Caribbean."[3]

The Greater Caribbean is an especially heterogeneous and fragmented region. Considering its expansive membership base comprises, for example, the "Group of Three" – Mexico, Colombia and Venezuela – as well as the mostly English-speaking members of CARICOM, formulating one coherent and unified perspective that adequately represents the region poses a significant challenge. However, inconsistencies among Member States need not be seen as antagonistic, and can therefore be overcome. The Association represents the merging of common needs among countries that have realized their regional similarities and historical ties, despite the diversity of their cultures, languages, sizes, political structures and economies.

Considering the region's tumultuous past, an important element that provoked the creation of the ACS was the recognition that the Greater Caribbean must be a zone for peace. At the time of the formation of the Association, all Member States – whether individually or collectively – were already deeply immersed in the globalisation process to improve their economic competitiveness; as such, the formation of an expanded and unified regional bloc was both desirable and advantageous. A major factor guiding this formation was the acknowledgement that integration and competitiveness would not be successful without regional stability, as the negative effects of conflict are a major impediment to economic and social development.

The recent tenth anniversary of the ACS is an occasion for reflection on the benefits that arise from the diversity of the region. One must see the ACS as an opportunity to engage a diverse sub-region in activities of cooperation and collaboration. Potential challenges to stability – whether internal or cross-border – mount significant obstacles to its main goals of regional integration and autonomy from external hegemony. Building a culture of peace and preventing violent conflict, therefore, is inextricably linked to the success of sustainable development in the Greater Caribbean, and the ACS, with its broad membership base and increasing focus on economic integration and cooperation, is a unique forum in which to present this challenge.

As such, the following article includes a brief overview of current ACS projects related to sustainable development, emphasizing the Association's focus on multilateralism and cooperation with related organisations in the region. The majority centers on the ACS's external partnerships for peace-building, especially its recent involvement with an international consortium, the Initiative for Conflict Prevention Through Quiet Diplomacy.

Current Issues and Initiatives –
Trade, Tourism, Transport, and Natural Disasters

As Federico Mayor noted a decade ago at the Second International Forum on the Culture of Peace, "There can be no peace without development and no development without peace."[4] The main goal of the ACS, as an organisation founded to achieve sustained cultural, economic, social, scientific and technological advancement, is to incorporate the promotion of sustainable development practices into the four areas of its integration scheme: trade, tourism, transport and natural disasters.[5]

With regard to trade, the ACS has focused its efforts on advancing programmes that target vulnerability to external factors and that aim to equalize the Member States and improve all States' capacity to negotiate with current or potential trading partners. A 2003 joint ACS study with the UN Economic Commission of Latin America and the Caribbean (ECLAC) found that the excessive dependence on a small number of exports has rendered most ACS countries more vulnerable to external factors and instability and have compromised their capacity to achieve sustained and sustainable growth.[6] As a result, sub-regional groups are anxious to deepen their respective integration schemes and to expand their economic relations within the Greater Caribbean in such a manner so as to reap maximum benefits from geographic proximity and similar levels of development. ACS Members are working on establishing partial free trade areas or preferential trade areas, which could lead the region toward a generalized free trade system.

There have also been efforts toward activities that reaffirm the regional position in external negotiations. Since the 3rd Summit in 2001, the ACS has been working on the issue of Special and Differential Treatment, especially on strategies whereby ACS Member States could be afforded concessions during Free Trade Area of the Americas (FTAA) negotiations. This is specifically applicable to the treatment of small economies, and the ACS has promoted studies on reducing the vulnerabilities of Member States that fall within this group. Research on the preparedness of small economies for globalisation and seminar workshops on trade negotiations and language training are additional efforts toward equilibrium of Member States.

The tourism sector is the most important source of foreign direct investment in the region, the most significant provider of employment and foreign exchange earnings for many ACS Member States, and represents the largest percentage of GDP earnings for the majority of the insular Caribbean. Furthermore, tourism has a multiplying effect on the remaining focal areas of the ACS, which is vitally important for the economic development of the region. At the same time, tourism is no doubt the most vulnerable to instability and conflict. As such, incorporating cooperative projects in areas that recognize the importance of tourist safety and language training are key elements to realizing the potential of the tourism sector.

A notable development in the inter-institutional cooperation process was the legal and operational collaboration between the ACS Secretariat and the Caribbean Tourism Organisation (CTO); the two organisations have agreed to jointly coordinate the Annual Caribbean Conference on Sustainable Tourism Development, the next which is schedule for May 2006 in Puerto Rico. This increased cooperation between the ACS and the CTO will bolster the Convention Establishing the Sustainable Tourism Zone of the Caribbean, which provides the legal basis for making the Caribbean known in the international arena as the first sustainable tourism zone in the world, promotes multi-destination tourism in the region, and raises standards and practices within the industry in environmental, economic, social and cultural areas.

The tourism sector is wholly dependent on the efficient functioning of other sectors of the ACS. Due essentially to its impact on tourism (and trade) within the region, an ECLAC study confirmed that international transport is a vital element for the economic activities of ACS countries.[7] The difficulties imposed by the current situation in both air and maritime transport constitute obstacles to the strengthening of regional ties. In response to these difficulties, the ACS established the programme "Uniting the Caribbean by Air and Sea" and has put forward memoranda of understanding and information-sharing databases to increase communication and cooperation among Member States.

Regional cooperation is also critical for the prevention and management of natural disasters. The objective being targeted by an ACS agreement for regional cooperation is to develop a network of legally binding mechanisms to promote cooperation for the prevention of natural disasters, through collaboration among the contracting parties and associated organisations within the region. Efforts must also be undertaken to strengthen the national bodies and domestic organisations responsible for disaster management, including providing them with the tools, technology and resources required to handle all steps of the disaster management cycle, such as prevention, mitigation and management, and emergency and relief services. In this respect, cooperative alliances, such as with the World Meteorological Organization, are critical.

As a brief outline of current issues and initiatives in the areas of trade, tourism, transport and natural disasters demonstrates, multilateral cooperation is crucial to the functioning of the Association. Efforts to preserve the common patrimony of the Caribbean Sea guide this cooperation. The ACS has been a leader in initiatives to ensure that the Caribbean Sea is recognized as a Special Area in the context of Sustainable Development.[8] This recognition will have exponential benefits for the success of all the ACS sectors in achieving regional integration and sustained development practices. Defining the Caribbean Sea as a Special Area identifies it as a common source of identity and functional space for all Member States that ignores linguistic, cultural and political divisions. It is the centerpiece of region-wide policies and mechanisms that facilitates agreement and collaboration.

Association of Caribbean States

Multilateralism, Cooperation and National Legitimacy

As mentioned, the set of countries comprising the Greater Caribbean is diverse with each Member State involved in a myriad of other regional arrangements, which can be seen as an opportunity for multilateral action and cooperation with other supranational organisations. The Declaration of Principles and Plan of Action of the ACS are firm in their commitment for collaboration with the United Nations and the World Trade Organisation. In addition, the ACS places great importance on developing a network of cooperative relations with its Founding Observers – CARICOM, CTO, ECLAC, the Secretariat for Central American Economic Integration (SIECA), the Central American Integration System (SICA), and the Latin American Economic System (SELA) – and with other organisations like the Andean Community of Nations (CAN), the Caribbean Regional Negotiating Machinery (CRNM), the Organisation of American States (OAS) and the Organisation of Eastern Caribbean States (OECS). The status of Founding Observer indicates a privileged status within the ACS, which surpasses that of Observers and other cooperation agents. Because the membership base is so large, the majority of ACS Member States are also members of other regional arrangements, many of which overlap as Founding Observers – such as the OAS, the North American Free Trade Agreement (NAFTA), CAN, CARICOM, and SICA – and have been involved in efforts to expand the FTAA and to create the South American Community of Nations (SACN).

Through linkages with other such supranational organisations the development of a culture of peace is significantly enhanced. Yet, while multilateralism has certainly become a trend in the Greater Caribbean, the potential for effective multilateral action is dependent on efficiency and legitimacy at the national level. Given the crisis of the model of the intervening State, greater importance has been placed on the relationship between government and society, with the understanding that they had to mutually recognize each other as actors involved in political action. According to Antonio Camou, the study of political relations from the perspective of governance refers to the quality of governments, taking into account their efficacy, efficiency, legitimacy, and their obligation to provide better living conditions for citizens.[9] The essence of good governance guarantees a balance between State and society and obligates the State to guarantee stability, bearing in mind social demands and avoiding social conflicts. In that respect, the notion of shared responsibility is necessary as a civic practice, which frees citizens from their status as subjects. Thus, political pluralism is maintained on the basis that democratic agreement of nations and governmental exercise is not a justification for force, but rather a process of building consensus. Furthermore, this new wave of politics has highlighted the importance of managing a system of ethical values associated with respect for social and economic rights, transparency, accountability and the fight against corruption. In this respect, the ACS Secretariat tries to foster an environment for countries of the Greater Caribbean to develop activities that fortify national legitimacy and good governance, and thus generate stability.

External Partnerships and Consortiums for Peace-building

It should be made clear that the ACS was not established as an organisation with a "political" mandate, but rather primarily for "consultation, cooperation and concerted action" addressing issues of the globalization of the international economy and progressive liberalization of hemispheric trade relations. This limits the capacity of the organisation to act in potentially violent conflict-related matters of the state, and may lessen the importance of the organisation at the national political level. As such, partnerships with other organisations and participation in consortiums involved in building a culture of peace – whether inter-governmental or civil society – are critical to advancing a peace-building agenda. Indeed, it is at least prima facie legitimate for the ACS to take up, on a consultative, cooperative and concerted basis, such issues which may affect stability in the region and thereby undermine economic and social development.[10]

UNESCO's Culture of Peace Concept

When developing a programme for the culture of peace in the Greater Caribbean, one can only look first to UNESCO, whose mission is to use education, science, and culture to create conditions for peace. The concept can be understood as shared values, attitudes, and behaviors based on non-violence and respect for fundamental rights and freedoms, understanding, tolerance and solidarity. It originates from participation, empowerment of the marginalized, and on the sharing and free flow of information, and maintains that "peace is not only the absence of conflict, but requires a positive, dynamic participatory process where dialogue is encouraged and conflicts are solved in a spirit of mutual understanding and cooperation."[11] Per the vision of UNESCO, conflict arising from diversity may be positive when confronted by active, non-violent responses that promote the transformation of violent competition into cooperation for shared goals, and culture of peace programming refers to the vision and process of collaboration among governments and civil society.[12]

Since the early 1990s – after former UN Secretary General Boutros-Ghali put forward "An Agenda for Peace" – a programme on a culture of peace emerged as the UN was trying to promote a climate of reconciliation after violence manifested in civil rather than inter-state conflict. Examples of UNESCO's work throughout the 1990s were its national programmes in post-Cold War Central America, where it established public confidence in democratic institutions through education campaigns and convinced conflicting parties to dialogue. The functions of UNESCO's programmes are to coordinate, in an integrated manner with other UN bodies, governmental bodies, and NGOs, the development of a methodology for peace based on cultural values. This includes efforts in the fields of education, science and technology in regards to developing behavior and values towards peace, as well as linking the concept of a culture of peace to democracy and sovereignty.[13] It is for this reason that the ACS Secretariat would like to form a partnership with UNESCO for current and future projects. UNESCO was a key collaborator on a recent workshop on building a culture of peace, and will be instrumental in a regional seminar on implementing a conflict prevention initiative in the Greater Caribbean, discussed below.

Civil Society Involvement

Engagement with civil society is central both to building a culture of peace and, more generally, to achieving the ACS's objective of regional stability as a basis for economic and social development. There are currently various movements spearheaded by non-governmental organisations focused on the sustainability of regional integration by taking into account, for example, human rights and environmental issues. Certainly, one fundamental way to move a culture of peace agenda forward and ensure its success is to involve civil society. By being less bureaucratic and more flexible than the existing official structures, these movements are well-placed to promote a social agenda within integration processes at the popular level.[14]

However, because of the formal organisational structure of the ACS consisting of two component parts, the Secretariat and the Ministerial Council, grassroots initiatives are not particularly well-represented and there are inherent limitations as to which social actors will participate in decision-making. Although delegates from NGOs and founding observer groups may attend committee meetings, and although work programmes and memoranda of understanding and cooperation have been signed with many regional organisations, these efforts so far focus largely on economic development, liberal trade, and transfers of technical competence, rather than social development, governance, and community-building issues.[15]

For many ACS decision-makers, civil society in the contemporary Caribbean context mostly signifies a heightened role for the private sector in the state. Although a new type of civil society has emerged within the Caribbean in response to such issues as political rights, gender equality, and indigenous demands and rights, these actors have generally not participated in making decisions about the processes of regional integration. There is therefore a need to broaden the scope of the social partners and create or fortify ties with NGOs and international organisations that have a social development mandate.

One of the ACS's social partners, La Coordinadora Regional de Investigaciones Económicas y Sociales (CRIES), in conjunction with La Facultad Latinoamericana de Ciencias Sociales (FLACSO), is engaged in activities related to the sustainability of integration by linking it to issues of potential conflict. For example, a recent project by CRIES and FLACSO promotes the development of a joint programme involving scholars and civil society organisations which approaches peace and security as "public goods," indicating a shift in paradigm where regional security is perceived, not as the ultimate goal, but as an "instrument" for conflict prevention and peace-building through improvements in governance and social and ethnic equality.[16]

Representatives from CRIES have recognized a "deficit" of civil society participation within the general framework of the security debate of regional organisations. They have recommended a more proactive approach that allows for the development of public policy follow-up and assessment programmes, as well as increased involvement in early-warning and confidence-building initiatives. This would also apply to "soft" security, such as peace-building efforts directed at sustainable economic and social development. Possible projects include: the design of community based conflict prevention programmes, including early-warning/diagnostic capabilities emphasizing root causes of conflict; implementing preventive mechanisms, such as dialogue and negotiation; monitoring likely "hotbeds" of local, national or regional conflict and; dissemination of early warning signs through a regional observatory which links community based initiatives with regional network lobbying and advocacy capacity. In order to advance a peace-building agenda, it is advantageous to strengthen ties with ACS social partners such as CRIES, using them as a vehicle to implement some of these conflict prevention initiatives.

The shift in paradigm – whereby the concept of security is broadened and deepened in terms of a "public good" and where peace-building is a broad-based socio-cultural project undertaken at all levels (local, national and regional) – implies the progressive inclusion of more civil society organisations and representatives in programmes, projects and eventually decision-making processes. The compelling logic of this follows from evidence that contributions of those most directly affected will yield better governance, social stability and economic prosperity. Simply, the people are not objects of governance or of development, but rather sentient and interested subjects whose participation is both morally required and necessary for fully informed decision-making and generating effective policy and law that avoids, reduces, or even resolves conflicts.

Managing Intra-Caribbean Migration

Within the context of developing a multilateral system of institutions and mechanisms devoted to building a culture of peace in the Greater Caribbean, intra-regional migration has been identified as a key issue. Indeed, transnational migration is a trend that can only be managed by cooperative regimes, thereby necessitating the collaboration of external partners and community representatives. Caused by various push and pull factors, this increasing movement and mixing of people is creating social and economic pressures which have the potential to evolve into tensions within and between States, affecting stability and development in the region. So far, little policy-oriented thinking has been directed towards the better ordering and management of such migration with a view, not only to preventing violent conflict, but to managing migration in a law-respecting and constructive manner through cooperative arrangements involving governmental authorities and interested civil society organisations.

Of prime importance is identifying and analyzing the current issues affecting the region. With the collaboration of the International Organisation for Migration (IOM) and the international NGO Human Rights Internet, the ACS has engaged scholars and policy-makers to comment on various aspects of intra-regional migration and conflict potential, with the intention to publish a book of approximately ten chapters, followed by a book launch. The publication will be groundbreaking in that it will be the first volume devoted exclusively to assessing the linkage between intra-regional migration and potentially violent conflict in the Greater Caribbean. As such, the compilation will not focus on the Caribbean diaspora, but current migration trends and themes within the Greater Caribbean that pose challenges to stability and development. Moreover, the expertise of local scholars and practitioners enhances the intra-Caribbean perspective.

In preparation for the publication, contributors have participated in a colloquium in San José, Costa Rica in July 2005 at the University for Peace of the United Nations, including an informal presentation of research topics and an inter-active dialogue about the themes addressed in the publication. Following the publication, a book launch will take place at the ACS Secretariat in Port of Spain, Trinidad in conjunction with the fourth annual IOM/UNHCR Joint Regional Seminar, to be co-hosted by the ACS. Representatives from a range of governments and civil society organisations will be invited to this event, not only to invite their comment but to stimulate their engagement in follow-up activities.

The ultimate goal of the intra-Caribbean migration publication and related endeavors is to stimulate policy development, including recommendations for concrete action, through informed debate about the relationship between intra-regional migration and potential conflict. The compilation is to be published in the three languages of the ACS – English, Spanish and French – thereby increasing the availability of migration/conflict-related scholarship and popular accessibility. Managing migration within the region is essential to maintaining stability and ensuring sustainable development practices. Successful action will ultimately be required at all levels and with the engagement of all segments of society.

Preventing Conflict Globally

As explained, the building of a culture of peace, and more specifically, developing a conflict prevention mechanism for the ACS, is dependent on external partnerships. Therefore, the ACS is collaborating with the Initiative on Conflict Prevention Through

Quiet Diplomacy, an international consortium on conflict prevention originally based on the experience of the High Commissioner on National Minorities (HCNM) of the Organisation for Security and Cooperation in Europe (OSCE), which grew out of transitions across Europe.

The Initiative is in part an outgrowth of expert consultations and briefings that began in 2001, which brought together senior practitioners from the UN, regional and sub-regional inter-governmental organisations, as well as leading academic and NGO experts from both the human rights and conflict resolution fields to consider the possibilities for pursuing new institutional mechanisms for early engagement in situations with the potential to lead to violent conflict. The overriding conclusions at these meetings have been that regional inter-governmental organisations, when provided with adequate mandates and resources, can effectively address the root causes of violent conflict through early preventive action and co-operative engagement and, that such arrangements enhance rather than threaten the role of the State as an effective actor in addressing non-traditional security threats.

The Initiative is aimed at preventing violent conflict through quiet diplomatic arrangements within existing regional and sub-regional inter-governmental organisations. The rationale for such arrangements is as follows. Violent conflict, whether spontaneous or organized, causes enormous human and material losses throughout the world, and gives rise to tremendous costs for post-conflict peace-building, including physical reconstruction and social rehabilitation. It is obvious that prevention of such losses and subsequent costs is desirable, if not increasingly imperative, in both human and financial terms. Prevention of violent conflict is also vital to sustainable economic and social development, including through trade, tourism, transport and productive cultural exchange. Addressing the causes of conflict – both root and proximate – is beneficial to productive policy-making. Some such causes are by their nature international and, thus, require international cooperation if responses are to be effective.

As the situations in Haiti and Colombia show, by the time violence breaks out, a conflict has developed its own dynamics, and the chances for successful diplomatic engagement are substantially reduced, largely leaving the international community with costly options and uncertain outcomes from other kinds of intervention. Thus, in order to prevent such unwelcome developments, co-operative action must come much earlier. For this, pre-standing mechanisms with appropriate mandates and resources are required. The official machinery of the international community offers little in the way of institutions or mechanisms with a mandate to effectively address root causes at an early stage.

Although the OAS has well-established mechanisms for the pacific settlement of disputes – the normative framework of the 1948 Bogotá Pact and the operational mechanism of the OAS Permanent Council, for example – and has made progress on an increased security agenda with the establishment of the Committee on Hemispheric Security, these measures focus on inter-state conflicts that are in most cases already of a violent nature. The Inter-American Commission on Human Rights (in conjunction with the Inter-American Court) does contribute to the prevention of conflicts in the region through its monitoring, fact-finding, and recommendations to Member States regarding individual human rights violations, but major obstacles preclude its efficient functioning. The Commission's "state of affairs," characterized by a lack of resources and the OAS's hesitancy to respond to the Commission's denunciations because of internal political concerns, "is hardly conducive to systematic early warning or conflict-awareness raising."[17]

The Relevance of the OSCE High Commissioner on National Minorities

Surprisingly, the only institution dedicated to address such potential conflict – involving ethnic divisions or inter-community disputes which affect relations among States – has been the OSCE High Commissioner on National Minorities, established in 1992 to address inter-ethnic conflicts affecting OSCE States.[18] It has repeatedly been argued that the function and experience of the OSCE High Commissioner on National Minorities provides a promising example of especially pre-conflict preventive action. Indeed, UN Secretary-General Kofi Annan has argued that other regional organisations would do well to follow the example of the OSCE and consider establishing similar institutions.[19]

The method developed by the first HCNM, Mr. Max van der Stoel (Netherlands), was a problem-solving approach that combines quiet diplomacy, policy advice and technical (often legal) assistance. In addition, it includes a certain amount of education of policy-makers and law-makers with respect to norms and practices and the practical consequences of leaving problems unaddressed or unsolved. The approach is fundamentally flexible, open to a wide variety of tools and approaches depending on the context, and within the constraints of both a normative and security-conscious basis for action. In the HCNM's work, such solutions and steps have included provision of advice on, for example: policy and law on issues of the use of language(s), education, cultural policy and financing, economic development policies and projects, political participation, elections, decentralization, constitutional reform, citizenship policies, and bilateral relations, including the conclusion and effective implementation of treaties. It is argued that the HCNM framework offers significant experience of pre-conflict preventive diplomacy from which others could learn.[20]

Application to the Greater Caribbean

As the HCNM is unique in the field, it seems logical to consider whether and how the successes of the HCNM approach might hold lessons for the Greater Caribbean. Because the ACS does not have an express political mandate, it must therefore advance programmes in terms of its own organisational scope focusing on economic and social development. It is effective to do so through partnerships and synergies with civil society and other intergovernmental organisations that have already developed concepts and instruments.

From this perspective, Human Rights Internet has partnered with the ACS to advance programmes on conflict prevention through the Greater Caribbean component of the Initiative on Conflict Prevention Through Quiet Diplomacy. The first joint activity, with collaboration from UNESCO, was a workshop on "Building a Culture of Peace and Preventing Conflict in the Greater Caribbean," that took place in January 2005 in Port of Spain at the ACS Secretariat. Additional collaboration on this and related initiatives have come from the United Nations Development Programme, ECLAC, CRIES, FLACSO, and the University of the West Indies (St. Augustine). The purpose of this meeting was to consider conflict potential affecting relations between states within the Greater Caribbean and to identify issues which could benefit from lessons to be drawn from the OSCE experience with its quiet diplomatic, human rights-informed, root causes, problem-solving approach. In follow-up, a regional conference was held in September 2005, and hosted by the Government of the Dominican Republic.

While this meeting included a brief presentation on the unique OSCE approach, it is clear that the Caribbean context is in many ways distinct from that in Europe.

The intent, therefore, was to gather a group of experts from varying backgrounds to discuss and debate how the region might address its own problems and build a culture of peace. The overarching goal of this initiative is to create regional awareness among governments and civil society of the need to develop a multilateral system, specific to the Greater Caribbean, aimed at preventing conflict through quiet diplomacy. Expected results include: increased knowledge among governments and civil society organisations (non-profit and for profit) regarding the possible tools to deal with conflict at the earliest stage, before violence erupts; engagement with governments and civil society organisations of the Caribbean region aimed at fostering a culture of peace and raising their interest in the creation of appropriate sub-regional structures for early preventive diplomacy; and shaping a vision of a culture of peace in the Caribbean, and outlining concrete follow-up, including institutional capacity-building.

Efforts put forth thus far by initiatives in the Greater Caribbean have centered on fortifying the commitment of non-governmental actors and promoting joint on-going activities on conflict prevention so as to promote a collaborative approach and not duplicate efforts. With the participation of universities, non-governmental organisations, and UN representatives, the January 2005 workshop laid the foundation for future engagement of countries in the Greater Caribbean. The strategy is that the support of carefully-selected representatives of these organisations will help build future partnerships with responsible authorities at the governmental level. Once these partnerships have been formed, further initiatives will seek to aid countries of the region build institutional capacity in areas of governance, early warning of threats to stability, and multilateral negotiation, thereby creating conditions for sustainable peace and development.

Conclusion

In developing support for a conflict prevention initiative in the Greater Caribbean, the main interest proceeds from the link between security and stability, which is vital to avoid costly loss of life and property and for stimulating economic development through liberalized trade and other cooperative exchanges. Social unrest or violent conflict severely hampers the ability of the region to function and develop in terms of the main areas of the ACS – trade, tourism, transport and natural disasters. Some have argued that social equity and a strong civil society within the region can only be achieved by first improving economic opportunity. Yet although ACS has made progress in meeting the goals of a liberalized trade agenda, the social and cultural elements of social development have not simply followed suit. Therefore, through an early and quiet problem-solving approach, ACS partnerships with external actors will help foster an environment that will enable the building a culture of peace and prevention of conflict in the Greater Caribbean. This in turn is the basis for sustainable development with economic and social prosperity. Certainly, there is every reason to try to construct such a future for all those in the region.

References

Kofi Annan, UN Secretary General's Statement at the Sixth OSCE Summit, Istanbul, November 18–19, 1999.

Association of Caribbean States, Convention Establishing the Association of Caribbean States, Port of Spain, Trinidad and Tobago, July 1994.

"Declaration of Principles and Plan of Action on Tourism, Trade and Transportation," Inaugural Summit of Heads of State and Government and Representatives of the States, Countries and Territories of the Association of Caribbean States, Port of Spain, Trinidad and Tobago, August 17–18, 1995.

"Framework Paper-Toward a New Vision of the Association of Caribbean States," Preparatory Meeting and Tenth Ordinary Meeting of the Ministerial Council, December 14–15, 2004, Port of Spain, Trinidad and Tobago. ACS/2004/CM.X/INF.011

Baranyi, Stephen, "Inter-American Institutions and Conflict Prevention," FOCAL Policy Paper, March 2005.

Camou, Antonio, "Los Desafíos de la Gobernabilidad," estudio preliminar y compilación. FLACSO/Mexico, UNAM y Plaza y Yanes, eds. México, 2001.

Comisión Económica para América Latina /Association of Caribbean States, "Las Tendencias Principales del Comercio, Política Comercial e Integración en el Gran Caribe,"30 de octubre, 2003. LC/CAR/G.756.

Girvan, Norman, "Reinterpreting the Caribbean," New Caribbean Thought, Folke Lindahl and Brian Meeks, eds. (University of West Indies Press: St. Augustine, Trinidad, 2001).

Jácome, Francine, Paz Millet and Andrés Serbin, "Conflict Prevention, Civil Society and International Organisations: The Difficult Path for Peace Building in Latin America and the Caribbean," FOCAL Policy Paper, March 2005.

Mayor, Federico, "Closing Address of the Second International Forum on the Culture of Peace (The Manila Forum)", November 26–30, 1995, Office of the Presidential Adviser on the Peace Process, Manila, Philippines.

Nicol, Heather, "The Association of Caribbean States and Sustainable Development: An Assessment," Social and Economic Studies 49:4 (2000).

Packer, John, "Briefing on Quiet Diplomatic Conflict Prevention: Towards New Institutional Arrangements," May 2, 2004, Discussion Paper, The Rockefeller Foundation, New York.

Packer, John, "The OSCE High Commissioner on National Minorities: Pyrometer, Prophylactic, Pyrosvestis," Minorities, Peoples and Self-Determination: Essays in Honour of Patrick Thornberry, Nazila Ghanea and Alexandra Xanthaki, eds. (Leiden/Boston: Martinus Nijhoff Publishers, 2005), 249–268.

Report of the West Indian Commission, Time for Action (The Press-University of the West Indies: Mona, Jamaica, 1993).

UN General Assembly, "Declaration and Progamme for Action on a Culture of Peace," Fifty-third session. A/53/L.79; See also UNGA Resolutions 51/101 and A/52/292.

UNESCO, "Framework for the Manila Forum,", Second International Forum on the Culture of Peace (The Manila Forum)", 26–30 November 1995, Office of the Presidential Adviser on the Peace Process, Manila, Philippines, 10.

"Hacia una Cultura Global de Paz," Documento de trabajo preparado por el Programa Cultura de Paz, Manila, las Filipinas, Noviembre 1995.

Notes

1   Recognizing CARICOM needs to widen and deepen its trade and economic linkages within the region, and having suffered considerably from economic decline during the 1980s, the West Indian Commission was established in 1989, which later recommended an organisation such as the ACS that would include an expanded membership base. For information on the origins of the ACS, see Report of the West Indian Commission, Time for Action (The Press-University of the West Indies: Mona, Jamaica, 1993). For more information on the mandate and current activities of the ACS see http://www.acs-aec.org/. For a comparison with CARICOM, see http://www.caricom.org/.

2   The "Caribbean Sea" is more of a political construct than a geographical reality; it is disputed that El Salvador, the Bahamas, Suriname and Guyana border the Sea.

3   The prevention and management of natural disasters was subsequently added to the work of the transport directorate.

4   Federico Mayor, "Closing Address of the Second International Forum on the Culture of Peace (The Manila Forum)", November 26–30, 1995, Office of the Presidential Adviser on the Peace Process, Manila, Philippines.

5   ACS projects explained in this section are taken from the "Framework Paper-Toward a New Vision of the Association of Caribbean States," Preparatory Meeting and Tenth Ordinary Meeting of the Ministerial Council, December 14–15, 2004, Port of Spain, Trinidad and Tobago. ACS/2004/CM.X/INF.011

6   Comisión Económica para América Latina /Asociación de Estados del Caribe, "Las Tendencias Principales del Comercio, Política Comercial e Integración en el Gran Caribe,"30 de octubre, 2003. LC/CAR/G.756.

7   Ibid.

8   Several drafts of resolutions declaring the Caribbean Sea a Special Area in the context of Sustainable Development have been submitted to the United Nations General Assembly, but none has been formally adopted.

9   Antonio Camou, "Los Desafíos de la Gobernabilidad," estudio preliminar y compilación. FLACSO/Mexico, UNAM y Plaza y Yanes, eds. México, 2001.

10 According to the convention that founded the ACS in 1994, the Association is to pursue the fulfillment of its purposes "progressively" through specified and evolving activities. Indeed, the Convention expressly foresees in Article III.2.f that engagement in "other areas as may be agreed upon" – as are consistent with its basic purposes and per the mandate of the organizational structure of the ACS – presumably as relations among ACS Members both broaden and deepen.

11 UN General Assembly, "Declaration and Progamme for Action on a Culture of Peace," Fifty-third session. A/53/L.79; See also UNGA Resolutions 51/101 and A/52/292.

12 UNESCO, "Framework for the Manila Forum,", Second International Forum on the Culture of Peace (The Manila Forum)" 26–30 November 1995, Office of the Presidential Adviser on the Peace Process, Manila, Philippines, 10.

13 UNESCO, "Hacia una Cultura Global de Paz," Documento de trabajo preparado por el Programmea Cultura de Paz, Manila, las Filipinas, noviembre 1995.

14 Norman Girvan, "Reinterpreting the Caribbean," New Caribbean Thought, Folke Lindahl and Brian Meeks, eds. (University of West Indies Press: 2001), 11.

15 Heather Nicol, "The Association of Caribbean States and Sustainable Development: An Assessment," Social and Economic Studies 49:4 (2000).

16 Francine Jácome, Paz Millet and Andrés Serbin, "Conflict Prevention, Civil Society and International Organisations: The Difficult Path for Peace Building in Latin America and the Caribbean," FOCAL Policy Paper, March 2005.

17 Stephen Baranyi, "Inter-American Institutions and Conflict Prevention," FOCAL Policy Paper, March 2005: 6.

18 For more information on the strategy and past examples of the OSCE's High Commissioner on National Minorities, see: http://www.osce.org/hcnm/. See also John Packer "The OSCE High Commissioner on National Minorities; Pyrometer, Prophylactic, Pyrosvestis," Minorities, Peoples and Self-Determination: Essays in Honour of Patrick Thornberry, Nazila Ghanea and Alexandra Xanthaki, eds. (Leiden/Boston: Martinus Nijhoff Publishers, 2005), 249–268.

19 Kofi Annan, UN Secretary General's Statement at the Sixth OSCE Summit, Istanbul, November 18–19, 1999.

20 John Packer, "Briefing on Quiet Diplomatic Conflict Prevention: Towards New Institutional Arrangements," May 2, 2004, Discussion Paper, The Rockefeller Foundation, New York.

ASSOCIATION
OF SOUTHEAST ASIAN NATIONS

ASSOCIATION OF SOUTHEAST ASIAN NATIONS

Establishment

The Association of Southeast Asian Nations or ASEAN was established on 8 August 1967 in Bangkok by the five original Member Countries, namely Indonesia, Malaysia, Philippines, Singapore, and Thailand. Brunei Darussalam joined on 8 January 1984, Vietnam on 28 July 1995, Laos and Myanmar on 23 July 1997, and Cambodia on 30 April 1999.

ASEAN is headquartered in Jakarta, Indonesia.

Executive Head

H. E. Mr. Ong Keng Yong, Secretary-General of ASEAN

Objectives

The ASEAN Declaration states that the aims and purposes of the Association are:

– To accelerate the economic growth, social progress and cultural development in the region through joint endeavours in the spirit of equality and partnership in order to strengthen the foundation for a prosperous and peaceful community of Southeast Asian nations, and

– To promote regional peace and stability through abiding respect for justice and the rule of law in the relationship among countries in the region and adherence to the principles of the United Nations Charter.

In 1992, the ASEAN Heads of State and Government declared that ASEAN should intensify its external dialogues in political and security matters as a means of building cooperative ties with States in the Asia-Pacific region. Two years later, the ASEAN Regional Forum or ARF was established. The ARF aims to promote confidence building, preventive diplomacy and conflict resolution in the region.

The present participants in the ARF include: Australia, Brunei Darussalam, Cambodia, Canada, China, European Union, India, Indonesia, Japan, Democratic Peoples' Republic of Korea, Republic of Korea, Laos, Malaysia, Myanmar, Mongolia, New Zealand, Pakistan, Papua New Guinea, Philippines, Russian Federation, Singapore, Thailand, United States, Viet Nam.

The ASEAN Security Community is envisaged to bring ASEAN's political and security cooperation to a higher plane to ensure that countries in the region live at peace with one another and with the world at large in a just, democratic and harmonious environment.

Through political dialogue and confidence building, no tension has escalated into armed confrontation among ASEAN Member States since its establishment.

Contact Information

Association of Southeast Asian Nations

70A, Jalan Sisingamangaraja
Jakarta 12110
Indonesia

Telephone: + 622 1 7262991
Fax: + 662 1 7398234

Internet: **http://www.aseansec.org**

ASEAN and the Culture of Peace

H. E. Mr. Ong Keng Yong, Secretary-General of ASEAN

1. The Association of Southeast Asian Nations (ASEAN) subscribes to the principles and objectives of the United Nations' Culture of Peace program. We share in the conviction that the Culture of Peace is a set of values, attitudes, modes of behaviour and ways of life that reject violence and prevent conflicts by tackling their root causes to solve problems through dialogue and negotiation among individuals, communities and nations.

2. At an ASEAN Summit, the Leaders of ASEAN have declared that, "Cooperative peace and shared prosperity shall be the fundamental goals of ASEAN." Therefore, our concept of peace is not passive but active peace. In fact, promotion of regional cooperation is among the six fundamental principles of inter-state relations, which has been agreed by ASEAN as reflected in the Treaty of Amity and Cooperation in Southeast Asia. The other fundamental principles include (a) Mutual respect for the independence, sovereignty, equality, territorial integrity and national identity of all nations; (b) The right of every State to lead its national existence free from external interference, subversion or coercion; (c) Non-interference in the internal affairs of one another; (d) Settlement of differences or disputes by peaceful means; and (e) Renunciation of the threat or use of force.

3. True to its commitment to promote peace and stability through regional cooperation, all ASEAN Member Countries actively participate in the four broad areas of political and security dialogue, economic cooperation and integration, functional cooperation and the promotion of external relations.

4. The promotion of peace and international understanding is a noble cause that could be an end in itself. But through cooperation and as the region becomes more economically integrated and interdependent, the Member Countries share even more stakes in the preservation of regional peace and stability. In other words, the culture of peace and the habit of cooperation could constitute into a virtuous cycle of mutually reinforcing norms.

5. ASEAN cannot be truly at peace unless the broader region, if not the whole world, is at peace. Thus, in recognition of our security interdependence, ASEAN has promoted diversified external relations with its neighbours as well as its traditional economic partners around the world. ASEAN now has built a network of what it calls Dialogue Partnership with ten countries, namely Australia, Canada, China, the European Union, India, Japan, Republic of Korea, New Zealand, the Russian Federation, and the United States. The United Nations Development Programme has also been accorded the same status as an institutional partner.

6. Established since 1994, the ASEAN Regional Forum (ARF) aims to develop confidence building measures, preventive diplomacy and, eventually, conflict resolution in the Asia Pacific. The ARF now consists of 24 participants, namely Australia, Brunei Darussalam, Cambodia, Canada, China, European Union, India, Indonesia, Japan, Democratic Peoples' Republic of Korea, Republic of Korea, Laos, Malaysia, Myanmar, Mongolia, New Zealand, Pakistan, Papua New Guinea, Philippines, Russian Federation, Singapore, Thailand, United States, Viet Nam.

7. Inter-state disputes remain in the ASEAN region. Like in human relations, they will probably persist as long as nations exist. Nevertheless, in a community of friendly, peace-loving and democratic states, conflicts and disputes do not go out of bounds. Adherence to certain principles and norms of behaviour contribute to ensuring that conflicts are managed, if not resolved, in a peaceful manner. Conflicts and disputes are placed in their proper and enlightened perspective.

8. The recently adopted ASEAN Security Community (ASC) will give an overarching framework and direction to ASEAN's commitment to building a zone of peace in Southeast Asia. As declared by the ASEAN Leaders, the ASC "will bring ASEAN's political and security cooperation to a higher plane to ensure that countries in the region live at peace with one another and with the world at large in a just, democratic and harmonious environment. The ASEAN Security Community members shall rely exclusively on peaceful processes in the settlement of intra-regional differences and regard their security as fundamentally linked to one another and bound by geographic location, common vision and objective."

9. The ASC indicates a beginning of a shift in the mindset from inter-governmental collaboration into a community of nations framework. The former is usually distinguished by immediate reciprocity while the latter has diffuse or long-term reciprocity and where national interests are identified more and more with the broader community interest.

10. In conclusion, we believe that the prospect of sustaining and strengthening the culture of peace in our region depends greatly on the prospect of building and nurturing a community of Southeast Asian nations.

BLACK SEA ECONOMIC COOPERATION ORGANIZATION

BLACK SEA ECONOMIC COOPERATION ORGANIZATION

Establishment

The Black Sea Economic Cooperation Organization (BSEC) is a regional organization of economic cooperation bringing together twelve countries contiguous to the Black Sea area, namely Albania, Armenia, Azerbaijan, Bulgaria, Georgia, Greece, Moldova, Romania, the Russian Federation, Turkey, Serbia and Montenegro, and Ukraine.

On the European landscape the BSEC is a relatively young multilateral institution. Its official birthday is 1 May 1999. This is the date of entering into force of the Charter of the BSEC, previously signed and ratified by all Member States, by which the Organization of the Black Sea Economic Cooperation acquired international legal identity.

The actual structure of the BSEC stemmed out from a process of cooperation, which was launched more than one decade ago, when the Heads of State and Government of the BSEC Participating States signed the Declaration on Black Sea Economic Cooperation at a Summit Meeting in Istanbul on 25 June 1992.

BSEC covers an area of nearly 20 million km^2, and serves an unsaturated market of 330 million people. The Black Sea region is after the Gulf, the second largest source of oil and natural gas.

The Organization of the Black Sea Economic Cooperation is headquartered in Istanbul, Turkey

Executive Head

H. E. Mr. Tedo Japaridze, Secretary-General of the BSEC

Objectives

The mission of the BSEC process is:

– To promote a climate conducive to a lasting and closer cooperation among the States of the BSEC Region;

– To establish a network of cooperation aimed at facilitating trade and economic development as well as scientific, cultural and human contacts in the region; and

– To develop the regional cooperation as a part of the integration process in Europe, based on human rights and fundamental freedoms, prosperity through economic liberty, social justice, and equal security and stability which is open for interaction with other countries, regional initiatives and international organizations and financial institutions.

Contact Information

Black Sea Economic Cooperation Organization

Permanent International Secretariat
Istinye Cad., Müsir Fuad Pasa Yalisi, Eski Tersane
34460 Istinye Istanbul
Turkey

Telephone: + 90 212 229 63 30
Fax: + 90 212 229 63 36

Internet: **http://www.bsec-organization.org**

Black Sea Economic Cooperation Organization
– Permanent International Secretariat –

H. E. Mr. Tugay Uluçevik,
Ambassador, First Deputy Secretary-General of the BSEC

The Organization of the Black Sea Economic Cooperation (BSEC) came into existence in 1992 as a political initiative for economic cooperation when the whole world was going through a tremendous change. In its existence of 13 years it has gradually but successfully transformed itself into a full-fledged international organization with the ratification of its Charter. By developing economic and trade relations between the Member States in the geography which consists of the Balkans, Caucasus and the Black Sea Littoral States, BSEC aims at contributing to regional and international peace, security, stability and welfare.

The wind of change continues to blow at the dawn of the 21st century at an increasing speed. The process of globalization is underway with all its consequences. The members of the international community are becoming increasingly interdependent in economic and technical terms. New dangers and new challenges are threatening them equally.

Upon the ratification of its Charter on 1 May 1999, the Organization of the Black Sea Economic Cooperation was born with an international legal identity on the international scene. This has been a clear signal to the outside world of the serious intentions of the Member States to transform BSEC into an integrated and reliable entity with which other international players can fruitfully interact.

The founding Members of the Organization are Albania, Armenia, Azerbaijan, Bulgaria, Georgia, the Hellenic Republic, Moldova, Romania, the Russian Federation, Turkey and Ukraine. Lately on 14 April 2004, Serbia and Montenegro became the 12th Member of the BSEC Organization.

At present, Egypt, France, Germany, Israel, Italy, Poland, Slovak Republic and Tunisia enjoy observer status in our Organization.

At its 54th session of the UN General Assembly, by its resolution 54/5 of 8 October

1999, the United Nations granted observer status to the Organization of the Black Sea Economic Cooperation. This has been a landmark development enabling BSEC to take its place in the family of international organizations. The UN General Assembly Resolution 55/211 of 20 December 2000, on the Cooperation between the United Nations and the Organization of the Black Sea Economic Cooperation opened up new avenues for BSEC to develop cooperation or working relationship with other organizations within the UN system and beyond. BSEC signed Cooperation Agreements with the UN Economic Commission for Europe (UNECE), UN Environment Programme (UNEP) and the UN Industrial Development Organization (UNIDO).

BSEC has also developed cooperation with the UN Food and Agriculture Organization (FAO), World Trade Organization (WTO) and World Bank. The work to establish a formal framework for cooperation between BSEC and FAO is in progress. The seminars and workshops which have so far been organized by BSEC in several member countries on various areas, including environment, transport, SMEs, investment promotion, energy, human resources development, agricultural development and food safety, etc. have all enjoyed valuable technical, financial and professional support from international organizations.

The BSEC Economic Agenda was adopted in April 2001. Its main goal is to strengthen, through a project-based approach, existing collaboration and expanding it into new fields, providing better economic integration of its members as an important prerequisite for inclusion of the BSEC region in a broader European Economic space.

In keeping with the project-based approach adopted in the BSEC Economic Agenda, the Project development Fund was established in October 2002. Its purpose is to facilitate the elaboration and promotion of projects with high regional cooperation and development impact in the BSEC region at the early stage of their conception.

The Fund is constituted on the principle of voluntary contributions from the BSEC Member States, Black Sea Trade and Development Bank and other BSEC Related Bodies and BSEC Observers. Contributions from outside donors are welcomed, provided that their sources are transparent and the conditions attached to them are consistent with the principles and objectives of the BSEC Organization.

It goes without saying that economy and security are closely related issues. A process of economic cooperation and development can only evolve successfully in a secure and stable environment. Whereas security has never been a static concept. Since the end of the Cold War, it has been extremely fluid and it seems that this will continue well into the 21st century.

BSEC, while carrying out its mission of contribution to regional security and stability through the promotion of a sound economic cooperation among its Member States, has not failed to address itself to the new threats directed to regional and international peace, security and stability.

There is today in the international community a growing awareness that terrorism and terrorism related issues such as organized crime, illicit trafficking of drugs, arms and radioactive materials and illegal border crossings together with the proliferation of weapons of mass destruction are the new threats that mankind must face.

As a regional economic organization, BSEC is not directly involved in peace-keeping and conflict management. It renders its contribution to peace and security through economic cooperation and by means of implementing the so-called "soft" security measures.

BSEC launched in 1997 the process of regular meetings of the Ministers of Interior of the Member States. The process resulted in the signing in 1998 of "the Agreement on Cooperation in combating crime, in particular in its organized forms". The Agreement entered into force in 1999 which was later complemented by its two Additional Protocols including the one on terrorism.

Under these international instruments the Member States of BSEC have undertaken to cooperate and exchange information also with the purpose of preventing, suppressing, detecting, disclosing and investigating of crimes, including, inter alia, illegal trafficking in weapons, ammunition and explosives, as well as biological, chemical and radiological weapons and nuclear and radioactive materials.

The BSEC Member States have also addressed themselves to illicit trafficking of narcotic drugs and psychotropic substances as well as to criminal activities related to migration.

Pursuant to the mandate given by the Heads of State or Government of the BSEC Member States in June 2002, the consideration of ways and means of enhancing contribution of BSEC to strengthening security and stability in the region is continuing by the relevant political bodies of BSEC.

On 25 June 2004, the Council of the Ministers of Foreign Affairs of BSEC met in a special session in Istanbul and adopted by consensus the "Statement on the BSEC Contribution to Security and Stability." In that Statement the BSEC Members denounced and condemned all acts of terrorism some of which have also been perpetrated over the past years in the territories of BSEC Member States. They stated that terrorism cannot be associated with any religion, ethnic group or geographic area and that there can be no justification for terrorism whatsoever.

Over the past decade, BSEC has become an integral part of the European political and economic landscape. It has developed cooperation with several international organizations and regional initiatives on the basis of complementarity, comparative advantage and subsidiarity.

The whole region of BSEC has become the immediate neighbor of the enlarged EU as of 1st May 2004. This, indeed, is a landmark development with far-reaching consequences. In retrospect, it would not be wrong to consider the process that was initiated in 1990, leading to the creation of BSEC, as a side effect of European integration. As a matter of fact, in designing BSEC as a regional cooperation project, the Member States have shared a common vision of their regional cooperation as a part of the integration process in Europe. They have also regarded the economic cooperation in the Black Sea region as a process conducive to their accession in a long-lasting partnership with the European Union. It goes without saying that the EU constitutes the main focus and one of the highest foreign policy priorities of all the BSEC Member States. In charting the future road of BSEC, its Member States act in earnest with the aim of establishing collaboration with the European Union and jointly forging the Black Sea Dimension of EU.

At present, one BSEC Member State is also the Member of EU. Three BSEC Members, namely, Bulgaria, Romania and Turkey, are expected to join EU as full Members in the near or not too distant future. Consequently, the boundaries of the enlarged EU will also cover a significant part of the BSEC region, including a long coastline of the Black Sea. Thus, EU will become a major Black Sea actor. We all accept that the emerging new European Architecture should be free from new dividing lines. BSEC can play a major role in providing the necessary links between the enlarged EU and those of the BSEC Member States which are not Members of EU. Moreover, BSEC can be instrumental in bringing about a comprehensive platform for cooperation between enlarged EU and the rest of the European space. Mention should also be made in this context that Black Sea region is becoming Europe's major transport and energy transfer corridor.

BSEC serves as a model of cooperation, bringing together countries belonging to different cultures and varying historic experience, through cooperative activities bridging differences and developing common vision for the future of the region. This will help BSEC assert its place and role in the new emerging European architecture.

BSEC will continue to play its role with determination in efforts to strengthen multi-lateral cooperation to meet the global challenges of this millennium.

COMMONWEALTH
OF INDEPENDENT STATES

COMMONWEALTH OF INDEPENDENT STATES

Establishment

On 8 December 1991 in Viskuli, Belarus, the leaders of Belarus, the Russian Federation and Ukraine have signed the Agreement on Establishment of the Commonwealth of Independent States (CIS). On 21 December 1991 in Alma-Ata, the Heads of States of eleven sovereign countries, namely Azerbaijan, Armenia, Belarus, Kazakstan, the Kyrgyz Republic, Moldova, the Russian Federation, Tajikistan, Turkmenistan, Uzbekistan and Ukraine, established on equality basis the Commonwealth of Independent States. The participants of the meeting have unanimously adopted the Alma-Ata Declaration, which confirmed the devotion of the former union republics to cooperate in various fields of external and international policies, and announced the guarantees for implementation of international commitments of the former Soviet Union. Later, in December 1993, the Commonwealth was joined by Georgia.

Thus, at present, the CIS comprises 12 young sovereign States.

The Commonwealth of Independent States is headquartered in Minsk, Belarus.

Executive Head

H. E. Mr. Vladimir Borisovich Rushaylo, Chairman of the CIS Executive Committee

Objectives

The Commonwealth of Independent States serves the further development and strengthening of relations of friendship, good neighborhood, international harmony, trust, mutual understanding and mutually beneficial cooperation between its Member States.

The Commonwealth of Independent States facilitates:

– the realization of cooperation in political, economic, environmental, humanitarian, cultural and other spheres;

– universal and balanced economic and social development of Member States under the framework of common economic space, interstate cooperation and integration;

– cooperation between Member States to ensure international peace and security;

– assistance for citizens of Member States in free interaction, contacts and movement in the Commonwealth of Independent States;

– mutual legal assistance and cooperation on other spheres of legal relations; and

– peaceful resolution of disputes and conflicts between States of the Commonwealth.

Contact Information

Commonwealth of Independent States

Executive Secretariat
17 Kirov Street
220000, Minsk
Belarus

Telephone: + 375 172 22 35 59
Fax: + 375 172 27 23 39

Internet: **http://www.ec-cis.org**

The Ideas of the Culture of Peace
in the Process of Formation of the Commonwealth of Independent States

H. E. Mr. Yuri Yarov, Former Chairman of the CIS Executive Committee

In the early XXIst century, humanity has still been living under the conditions of diverse social, ethnic, religious and other kinds of conflicts, which are often very likely to be transformed into military confrontation.

The end of the Cold War and of the ideology-related confrontation between the East and the West created more favorable conditions for the world community to advance towards the establishment of the culture of peace. However, unfortunately, the political biases, religious fanaticism and particularly, the gap between the so called rich and poor countries' living standards, are a fertile soil for various conflicts and hostility. They slow down the economic and social development, and makes a threat to stability and security on our common planet – the Earth. At the centuries' cutting edge, the world found itself confronted with new challenges – terrorism and drug's attack, the threat to a human being's living environment, resulting from natural and technogene catastrophes. Under those conditions, the main goal, formulated in the UNESCO Charter about sixty years ago, – to awake people's desire for building stable peace and security – is still vital today.

In this context the significance of establishment and existence of the Commonwealth of Independent States (CIS) becomes ever more vivid both for our region and the whole world. The political decisions on the CIS's establishment, signed in December 1991 in Viskuli and Alma-Ata, broke off the process of the USSR's chaotic decay and shaped up a new basis for cooperation between the participating states of the Commonwealth.

At the CIS Jubilee Summit on 30 November 2001 the heads of states, giving their due respect for the political role of the CIS in formation of the new independent states' sovereignty, of their mutual relations under emerging conditions, expressed the firm conviction that "the interaction within the CIS framework is solidly based on our countries' coinciding strive for sustainable and progressive socio-economic development, and decent integration into the world community." This position gave its positive results in development of the CIS states' economies.

Over the four subsequent years the GNP growth in the CIS made almost 40 %, and this is the basis for social and political stability of states.

Unfortunately, the collapse of a single state, for many reasons, resulted in transformation of the accumulated contradictions into armed conflicts. The most acute conflicts turned out in the Republic of Tajikistan in the Trans-Dniester region, in Abkhazia (Georgia), as well as around Nagorny Karabakh. Being a regional organization, the CIS undertakes certain measures to settle the conflicts in the territories of the Commonwealth participating states, in compliance with Chapter VII of the UN Charter.

It is noteworthy, that the system of preventing and settling conflicts, as well as the post-conflict building of peace, is in the process of its formation in the Commonwealth of Independent States. Nevertheless, the efforts made by the Commonwealth in cooperation with the relevant UN and OSCE structures succeeded in transferring the existing conflicts in a number of the CIS participating states from the stage of armed confrontation into the phase of a political dialogue, negotiations, the quest for compromises and solutions. Thus, in the Trans-Dniester region the agreement on cease fire has been in force since 21 July 1992, being in line with the Agreement on the principles of peaceful settlements of the armed conflict; in the conflict around Nagorny Karabakh since 12 May 1994 (as a result of Russia's mediation) sustainable cease fire has been established; on 14 May 1994 the Agreement on cease fire and separation of forces in the conflict zone in Abkhazia (Georgia) came into force; on 27 June 1997 the Tajik authorities and the opposition signed the Comprehensive agreement on peace and national accord in Tajikistan.

Certainly, the road to building democratic society and formation of tolerance and stability, the road to the culture of accord, prevention of conflicts, wars and crisis, is extremely intricate. Hence, the positive experience in peace-making, accumulated in the Commonwealth, seems to be quite significant for the entire world community and, at the same time, could become the basis for building civilized relationships between states, as well as at a regional level.

Nowadays the culture of peace and accord is vital both as a visualized strategy, and on the other hand – as a plan of actions. The key principle of such a plan should become the establishment of the culture of peace and tolerance in the context of comprehensive democratic reforms. In our view, one of the main tasks for the

Commonwealth of Independent States

contemporary world is to comprehend the concept of the culture of peace, to widely popularize it and make it part of people's mentality.

It is also very important to avoid treating the phrase "culture of peace" as a mere metaphor, a kind of cliché. On the other hand, the interaction between peoples and individuals should be based on a mutual interest to the history and culture, which is to be supported by corresponding state policy, bilateral and multilateral agreements and programs.

In this respect, the role of the Council for cultural cooperation of the CIS participating states has to be noted. The Council elaborates draft agreements and programs, and after having been signed at the level of heads of governments, these documents make a good starting point for interstate cooperation in the cultural sphere through better knowledge of each other, and the promotion of better mutual understanding. As examples, we should mention here the Decision on the conduct of the Falk Art Festival in February 2002 in Moscow, as part of the celebration of the tenth anniversary of the Commonwealth of Independent States, and, particularly, the Program of cooperation between the CIS participating states in cultural sphere, which envisages mutual participation in national events and joint cultural actions of international impact. Each of them is a unique brick in a ground for the culture of peace and mutual respect. One of those actions was a recent Scientific and Practical Conference "International dialogue in the post-soviet space in the context of globalization" (Kyiv, October 2003).

The very idea of the culture of peace comprises various levels and it seems to be expedient to frame some of them:

– universal human values, securing the firmness of individual's basic rights and freedoms and uniqueness of each culture;

– best practices of relations between countries and people, based on mutual respect, openness and tolerance;

– culture of mutual relations between countries, embodied in the activity of political and artistic elites;

– everyday culture of inter-ethnic interaction, affected by tourism, migration and other factors, which influence people's mentality;

– culture of interaction between various social and ethnic groups within countries, based on the principles of tolerance and the strive for a dialogue.

Much space in the culture of peace is given to a life-long education. Life is a process of teaching and learning. Our everyday behavior is the main lesson we teach others, including the generation to come. Building a strong democratic state and civilized interstate relations requires a high level of education, by which we understand not only certain knowledge, taken as a whole, but also the ability to be responsible for one's actions. There can be no democracy without education and, therefore, without it there can be no freedom and capability of self-expression.

Without education it is impossible to counteract contemporary threats, may it be poverty, starvation or epidemics, destruction of environment or local conflicts. This once again proves the strong tie between the culture of peace and education. Clear understanding of this tie is the footing for the activity of the Council for cooperation in the field of education of the CIS participating states – the traditional conferences of ministers of education of the Commonwealth countries.

Over many centuries of human history the argument of force had been dominating, not the force of persuasion, but the one of dictating one's will. The culture of peace envisages the dictatorship to be substituted by a dialogue, by understanding others, other perception of the world, by respect for other people's views. And this means, in its turn, openness, knowledge of other cultures, languages, traditions and religions. The very first article of the UNESCO Charter states that we build peace through education, science and culture. Consequently, peace, development and democracy make an interdependent triad, in which all the elements are mutually supplemented and strengthened.

This understanding is particularly important for us in the objectively existing and dynamically developing process of globalization, which must serve ever tightening interdependence of the human race, also through a dialogue among cultures and civilizations.

Commonwealth of Independent States

We must pass this understanding on to the younger generation; otherwise there will be no transnational motion in the development of interstate relations. That is why in the framework of the Commonwealth of Independent States we do our best to lay down the basis for such relationships right now. For this purpose we conduct large-scale actions, such as the International Sports Games for Juniors of the CIS participating states and the Baltic states (Moscow, 2002), the Youth Delphic Games of the CIS countries in 2004 and 2005 taking place in the capital cities of the Republic of Moldova and Ukraine respectively; and the Regional Youth Forum "Youth of the XXIst Century: Reality and Perspectives" in September 2003. The final address by the Forum participants to governments, public organizations and the youth of the Commonwealth stresses the necessity to create a sectoral Council for youth problems of the CIS countries. The implementation of this idea is in process now.

And this means, that the ideas of the culture of peace in the Commonwealth do have real perspectives.

EUROPEAN COMMISSION
EUROPEAN UNION

EUROPEAN COMMISSION – EUROPEAN UNION

Establishment

The historical roots of the European Union lie in the Second World War. The idea of European integration was conceived to prevent such killing and destruction from ever happening again. It was first proposed by the French Foreign Minister Robert Schuman in a speech on 9 May 1950. This date, the "birthday" of what is now the European Union – EU –, is celebrated annually as Europe Day. The European Union is a family of currently 25 democratic European countries, committed to working together for peace and prosperity.

Its Member States have set up common institutions to which they delegate some of their sovereignty so that decisions on specific matters of joint interest can be made democratically at European level. This pooling of sovereignty is also called "European integration".

The European Commission is one of the most prominent institution of the European Union. As the driving force and executive body of the EU, the Commission was created to represent the European interest common to all Member States of the Union. The Commission is an EU institution as well the college of Commissioners. One Commissioner from each Member State. Thus, the European Commission is comprised of a President and 24 Commissioners.

The European Commission is headquartered in Brussels, Belgium.

Executive Head

H. E. Mr. José Manuel Barroso, President of the European Commission

Objectives

The external relations of the Barroso Commission is based on three key basic propositions on the EU's role in the emerging world order. The EU is a global player;

it pursues a specific foreign policy philosophy which one could term "effective multi-lateralism"; and, thanks to its specific nature, the Union disposes of a wide range of foreign policy instruments which are particularly suited to respond to today's challenges. The President has established a Group of Commissioners, chaired by him, and in charge of six external relations services.

H. E. Dr. Benita Ferrero-Waldner is deputy chair of the Group of External Relations' Commissioners, and responsible for External Relations and European Neighbourhood Policy. She is responsible for two Commission Departments: External Relations and the Europe Aid Cooperation Office. The External Relations Commissioner co-ordinates the external relations activities of the Commission, and ensures that the Commission has a clear identity and a coherent approach in its external activities.

Contact Information

European Commission

Rue de la Loi 200
1049 Brussels
Belgium – EU

Telephone: + 32 2 29 81 299
Fax: + 32 2 29 81 297

Internet: **http://www.europa.eu.int**
               http://www.europa.eu.int/comm/world
               http://www.europa.eu.int/comm/external_relations/index.htm

The EU's Commitment to Multilateralism with the United Nations at its Core: Working Together for Peace

H. E. Dr. Benita Ferrero-Waldner, European Commissioner for External Relations and European Neighbourhood Policy

The European Union's commitment to multilateralism with the United Nations (UN) – the only truly universal multilateral organisation – at its core, is at the very heart of our external policy. This commitment is rooted in our conviction that the international community needs a strong and efficient multilateral system, founded on universal rules and values, to respond to crises, challenges and threats on the global level. The EU, as a global player, has a responsibility – one we take very seriously – to contribute to an effective multilateral system with multilateral institutions that function properly and are equipped to deal with the challenges of the 21st century.

The need to build an international order based on effective multilateralism is underlined as one of the strategic objectives of the European Security Strategy, which also states that "the fundamental framework for international relations is the United Nations Charter. Strengthening the United Nations, equipping it to fulfil its responsibilities and to act effectively, must be a European priority". The multilateral commitment of the EU was also clearly stressed in a Communication adopted by the European Commission in September 2003 on the European Union and the United Nations and the choice of multilateralism[1].

The EU's commitment to a multilateral approach in dealing with today's interlinked challenges of development, the environment, peace and security, human rights and democracy, was also at the heart of the EU's approach to the UN Summit[2] held in New York 14–16 September 2005. It continues to guide our approach to the follow-up to the Summit. From the very outset we put considerable effort into making the Summit a success, committing ourselves to increase development aid volumes and aid effectiveness; improve policy coherence; and focus on Africa. We talked to partners all over the world to build consensus, with the aim of making the UN stronger and better equipped to deal effectively with global challenges.

EU-UN Cooperation

Interaction and cooperation between the EU and the UN has increased steadily over the years. The EU played a key role in developing and implementing new UN instruments such as the Kyoto Protocol and the International Criminal Court, and took an active part in international conferences such as the one on Financing for development in Monterey in 2002 and the World Summit for Sustainable Development in Johannesburg in 2002.

The EU's commitment to the UN also translates into a major contribution to the UN's activities. It works with all UN bodies, agencies and programmes across virtually the whole range of UN activities, from development cooperation, peacemaking and peacekeeping, humanitarian assistance, fostering environmental sustainability, and promoting human rights around the world. In financial terms the EU's Member States jointly make the largest contribution to the UN system. They provide around 38% of the UN regular budget, more than two-fifths of the contribution to UN peacekeeping operations, and around 50 % of all UN Member State's contributions to UN funds and programmes. The European Community (EC)'s contribution to the UN has increased from around EUR 260 million in 2000 to around EUR 875 million in 2004, excluding humanitarian assistance. In the period 2003–2005 the EC allocated around EUR 1.57 billion to humanitarian crises, approximately EUR 225 million of which went to UN agency operations in support of refugees, returnees and internally displaced people (IDPs).

In recent years the EU has expanded its cooperation with the UN from development assistance, food aid and humanitarian assistance, to include conflict prevention, crisis management and the broader scope of peacebuilding.

Conflict prevention and crisis management lie at the intersection of development and security. The EU "reasserted (its) commitment to contribute to the objectives of the UN in conflict prevention and crisis management"[3], and many important political and operational steps have been taken to strengthen our partnership in these areas. We realise that EU actions in conflict prevention and crisis management need to be consistent with and complementary to decisions and frameworks developed by the UN. We also have more opportunities to work together, thanks to the development of the EU's Common Foreign and Security Policy/European Security and Defence Policy (CFSP/ESDP). This has significantly increased our options for engaging in

European Commission – European Union

the political, diplomatic and military spheres, and therefore contributing to the UN's work. As a result, in recent years the EU Police Mission in Bosnia and Herzegovina took over from the UN task force, and in the Democratic Republic of Congo MONUC took over from the "Artemis" EU military operation.

Over the years the EU and UN agendas in the field of peace and security have evolved in similar directions. We both believe we must address the underlying structural causes that can lead to, perpetuate or aggravate violent conflicts. We have strengthened our cooperation both at the country level and between headquarters. We regularly exchange information on policy, programming and project assessments. And wherever possible we identify possible joint activities on conflict prevention and peace-building. In September 2003 we signed the "Joint Declaration on EU-UN Co-operation in Crisis Management" which focuses on practical co-operation in the field of crisis management and related issues such as planning, training, communication and best practices.

EU-UN cooperation in crisis management is largely focused on Africa. The EU (and the European Community) is often the biggest donor to UN-managed post conflict reconstruction programmes, including in the Democratic Republic of Congo, the Ivory Coast, Liberia, Sudan, and Burundi. In addition, the cooperation between the EU and the African Union supports a growing move towards African-led Peace Support Operations which directly or indirectly substitute for UN (DPKO) peace-keeping missions.

EU Member States and the European Community (EC) are active players in peace-building all over the world. A substantial part of our work is done through cooperation with the UN. This includes support to peacekeeping operations, peace processes, peace negotiations and reconciliation efforts; Demobilization, Disarmament, Re-integration and Rehabilitation (DDRR); de-mining; security sector reform; civilian administration and good governance; democratization; strengthening the rule of law; justice reform; ensuring respect for human rights; children-related post-conflict assistance; institution building, independent media, and truth commissions; facilitating the transition from crisis situation to normal cooperation; addressing the degradation and exploitation of natural resources; tackling the proliferation of small and light weapons; and targeted economic and other measures such as relief, rehabilitation, reconstruction operations and development assistance. Trade-related measures have also played a critical role in addressing post-conflict challenges.

We are convinced that the international community needs to cooperate more effectively to ensure that the available resources for peacebuilding are used to the fullest and most efficient extent. We are very pleased that the UN Summit established a Peacebuilding Commission, one of our top priorities for the Summit, since this should make a real difference to our work to promote peace and sustainable development in countries and regions ravaged by conflict.

Major Threats to Peace and Human Security

The steps we have made towards better cooperation in conflict prevention, crisis management and peacebuilding are all the more important when we consider the dimension of the security threats we face. Chief amongst these are the proliferation of small arms and landmines, environmental degradation, and the exploitation of natural resources.

Small arms are sometimes described as the "weapons of mass destruction of the poor". The accumulation and proliferation of small arms and light weapons (SALW) constitutes a specific threat to security, human safety, and socio-economic development. Small arms are responsible for more deaths and injuries than any other category of weaponry, and are a particular threat to peace and sustainable development in Africa. The EU has therefore pushed the development of a legally binding international instrument to regulate the marking, tracing and illicit brokering of small arms and light weapons. We also pushed to integrate the destruction of SALW surpluses into demobilization, disarmament and reintegration processes in the run-up to the September 2005 UN Summit.

We adopted a Programme for Preventing and Combating Illicit Trafficking in Conventional Weapons in 1997, and a year later, an EU Code of Conduct on Arms Exports as well as a Joint Action on the EU's contribution to combating the destabilising accumulation and spread of small arms. In 2001, the EU played an active role at the UN Conference on Illicit Trade in Small Arms and Light Weapons in All Its Aspects, and the European Community became a signatory to the UN Protocol against the Illicit Manufacturing of and Trafficking in Firearms, Their Parts and Components and Ammunition. The European Community has supported SALW-related projects in most parts of the world.

Landmines are another persistent threat to human security. Supporting international mine action is an integral part of the EU's foreign policy, development cooperation and humanitarian assistance. Our objective is to reach the "Zero Victim Target", a world where no one will be injured or killed by landmines. We believe this is an achievable goal.

The world has come a long way since the 1997 Mine Ban Treaty[4]. There are now fewer victims, no transfers of landmines by states, large numbers of stockpiled mines (more than 31 million) have been destroyed, and mine action programmes have been successfully implemented in many affected countries. The European Community has steadily increased its financial support. Since 1997 total EU (Member States and the EC) support has reached the record figure of more than EUR 1 billion, close to half the total world-wide support to mine action in the same period. The UN is one of our key partners in Mine Action, where we collaborate in particular with the United Nations Mine Action Service (UNMAS) and the UNDP.

Environmental degradation is widely recognised as a global threat to security, and the link between the illicit exploitation of natural resources (such as diamonds or timber) and conflict has emerged as a common factor in some of the most brutal recent conflicts, particularly in Africa. Environmental issues must be integrated in conflict prevention, humanitarian assistance, peacebuilding and reconstruction activities.

We also believe that the monitoring of scarce, degraded, valuable and/or transboundary environmental resources must be strengthened, in particular in areas where they could trigger or contribute to a conflict or where a better common management could improve neighbourly relations. The EU can contribute to better monitoring, including through a joint initiative of the European Commission and the European Space Agency which aims to establish by 2008 a European capacity for global monitoring of environment and security (GMES).

Recently, both the UN Secretary General's High-level Panel on Threats, Challenges and Change and the Commission for Africa have underlined the need for action to prevent a range of commodities being used to fuel conflict. Specific multilateral initiatives such as the Kimberley Process Certification Scheme for diamonds have been a real success. The EC is a leading participant in this Process, which is making a crucial contribution to ensuring transparency and proper regulation of the diamond sector in many countries ravaged by diamond-fuelled conflict (such as Sierra Leone,

DRC, or Angola). It is a crucial element in the stabilization and reconstruction of many African countries affected by violent conflict in recent years.

Conclusion

The EU's commitment to multilateral action will continue to guide our action in promoting security and peace in the coming years. As a global player we have a responsibility to work together with our partners to address and find solutions to the challenges facing today's world. On behalf of the European Commission I am determined that we will continue to make every effort to contribute to an effective multilateral system, and to support and champion the UN and its reform process.

1 Communication from the Commission to the Council and the European Parliament on "The European Union and the United Nations: The choice of multilateralism", COM (2003) 526, 10 September 2003.

2 As an illustration, see the Commission's Communication to the Council and the European Parliament on "The 2005 UN Summit – Addressing the global challenges and making a success of the reformed UN", COM (2005) 259, 15 June 2005.

3 Conclusions of the meeting of the General Affairs and External Relations Council, 21 July 2003.

4 Convention on the Prohibition of the Use, Stockpiling, Production and Transfer of Anti-personnel Mines and on Their Destruction.

LEAGUE OF ARAB STATES

LEAGUE OF ARAB STATES

Establishment

The League of Arab States (LAS) is a voluntary association of independent countries whose peoples are mainly Arabic speaking.

The Egyptian government first proposed the Arab League in 1943. Egypt and some of the other Arab States wanted closer cooperation without the loss of self-rule that would result from total union. The original charter of the Arab League created a regional organization of sovereign States that was neither a union nor a federation.

The League of Arab States was founded in Cairo on March 22, 1945.

The Arab League is comprised of 22 Member States:
Algeria, Bahrain, Comoros, Djibouti, Egypt, Iraq, Jordan, Kuwait, Lebanon, Libya, Mauritania, Morocco, Oman, Palestine, Qatar, Saudi Arabia, Somalia, Sudan, Syria, Tunisia, United Arab Emirates, and Yemen.

The League of Arab States is headquartered in Cairo, Egypt.

Executive Head

H. E. Mr. Amre Mussa, Secretary-General of the League of Arab States

Objectives

The Arab League's purposes are to strengthen ties among the Member States, coordinate their policies, and promote their common interests.
The League of Arab States is involved in political, economic, cultural, and social programs designed to promote the interests of Member States. The Arab League has served as a forum for Member States to coordinate their policy positions and deliberate on matters of common concern, setting some Arab disputes and limiting conflicts in its region of influence.

The Arab League has served as a platform for the drafting and conclusion of almost all landmark documents promoting economic integration among Member States. It has played an important role in shaping school curricula, and preserving manuscripts and Arab cultural heritage. The League of Arab States has also fostered cultural exchanges between Member States, encouraged youth and sports programs, helped to advance the role of women in Arab societies, and promoted child welfare activities.

Contact Information

League of Arab States

Tahrir Square
Cairo
Arab Republic of Egypt

Telephone: + 20 2 5750511
Fax: + 20 2 5740331

Internet: **http://www.arableagueonline.org**

Towards a Culture of Peace: An Arab Perspective

H. E. Mr. Amre Mussa, Secretary-General of the League of Arab States

It took the world a very long time to recover from the destructive impact and dramatic consequences of two world wars as well as the implications of a cold war between the two super powers in the post World War Two era. These two world wars resulted in millions of deaths, disabilities and injuries. On the economic level, they cost billions of dollars, destroyed the infrastructure and crippled many nations. Furthermore, the ideological and political confrontation between East and West that brought about the tide of the Cold War also brought an arms race along with it.

These dramatic developments prompted the emergence of new thinking that shaped the political, social and economic scene of the world. However, on many occasions this new thinking was put into question and in some cases it was even ignored.

Sixty years after the world lay down its arms at the end of World War II, inter-state and intra-state violence has not diminished. On the contrary, violence, although of a different nature, escalated and our contemporary history provides ample evidence for this sad fact. Not only are the cycles of violence churning in most of the regions of the globe, but poverty, diseases, and underdevelopment seem to be constant maladies that accompany a troubled humanity.

Our world today confronts yet a new danger. A danger that started to spread in the early nineties by those who do not hesitate to proliferate visions that advocate for a culture of war and nurture disastrous conflict among civilizations hoping that global politics too will be aligned along cultural lines.

To address this threat and its potential negative consequences, the United Nations launched a series of initiatives among which are the UN Declaration and Program of Action on a Culture of Peace and the Global Agenda for Dialogue Among Civilizations. A number of mobilizing projects to foster a culture of peace and dialogue among civilizations were initiated. The spreading and implementation of these projects would ultimately promote freedom, civil liberties, progress, prosperity, and the rule of law. However, these principles still have a long way to go before they evolve into the realm of reality. Meanwhile, many regions around the world today remain deprived of the basic requirements of peace, let alone its culture.

Indeed, the development of a culture of peace is today a more urgent priority than ever before. However, developing and disseminating such a culture is a complex task that is essentially interlinked and interdependent with responsibilities in a number of spheres at the national and international levels while addressing both soft and hard security issues including human security, as well as addressing media-related dimensions and educational aspects.

To promote a culture of peace, the world does need a sound process of reform and just solutions to the major political problems, especially those threatening regional and international peace and security. It desperately needs sound economic and social development plans that would help poor countries see the light at the end of the long dark tunnel of underdevelopment. Needless to say, like all regions, the Arab world is much affected by these developments and has its requisites for advancement and its set of obstacles that impede its efforts towards development and progress.

A region in transition, developing, modernizing and building the foundation for its own renaissance, the Arab world, with its vast natural and human resources, is capable of achieving progress. But sustainable progress can not be attained in the absence of peace.

Undeniably, the Arab-Israeli conflict is one of the most tragic conflicts of our times. It is a conflict for which a peaceful end remains elusive. Our region has lived with the consequences of fifty years of Palestinian dispossession and continues to witness the daily experience of unrelenting difficulties and humiliation experienced by ordinary Palestinians under occupation. A whole people in our region live wretchedly under the eyes of the international community and the conflict remains unresolved. Does not this constitute a flagrant and manifest breach of numerous UN resolutions as well as the principles of human rights and international humanitarian law including the Fourth Geneva Convention?

The League of Arab States, in June 1996 at the Cairo Extra-Ordinary Arab Summit, unanimously resolved that a just and comprehensive peace in the Middle East is the strategic choice for the Arab world, provided that it could be achieved in accordance with international legality. In Beirut in 2002, the Arab Summit reaffirmed this commitment and unanimously adopted the Arab Peace Initiative which calls for the full Israeli withdrawal from the Arab territories occupied since June 1967, in implementation of Security Council Resolutions 242 and 338 which were reaffirmed by the

Madrid Conference of 1991, and Israel's acceptance of the establishment of an independent viable Palestinian state with East Jerusalem as its capital, in return for the establishment of normal relations in the context of a comprehensive peace with Israel. Israel has offered no positive response to this clear sign of Arab good will.

It is important to note, however, that no matter how central it is to the stability of the Middle East, the Arab-Israeli conflict is not the only crucial problem in this part of the world. The conflicts in parts of Sudan, the armed confrontations in Somalia and the situation in Iraq with all its complexity are equally disturbing to this region and to world peace and security at large.

There is a growing sense of frustration and despair among the peoples of the region because justice, as envisaged through the adherence to international law and the basic principles enshrined in the UN Charter, continues to be denied. The international community has to ask itself: can a culture of peace flourish when the principles of international law are being flouted, deliberately ignored or selectively applied?

The Arab region is a rich blend of many and diverse influences. It treasures a great heritage, and throughout its history, was home to various ethnic, linguistic and religious groups. Islam and the Arabic language constitute its two predominant cultural features. The fundamental tenets of Islam, and the richness of its teachings strongly advocate for the culture and achievement of peace.

Islam helped in the preservation of the teachings and knowledge of other civilizations and cultures, and contributed in the genesis of the renaissance. It successfully gathered and preserved the intellectual contribution of the Greek and Roman civilizations, and at the same time made its own valuable contribution to many fields of human endeavor, including medicine, science, mathematics, algebra, law, agriculture, theology, music, and astronomy. Islam helped to create the modern civilization that we are currently proud of. Its contribution is part and parcel of the current common heritage of mankind. Such multi-faceted contributions of the Islamic civilization to the history of mankind should not be ignored or under-estimated.

Regrettably, in recent years, some influential circles set to search for an enemy found their target in Islam. And in the aftermath of the 9/11, the world witnessed a surfacing of many voices accusing Islam of nourishing inherent hatred for the West. These voices have labeled Muslim societies as terrorist, backward and unjust societies fermenting intolerance and promoting violence. It is difficult to deny that some media institutions in the West played and continue to play a negative role in feeding the contemporary attack on Islam, capitalizing in some cases on sheer ignorance. The Muslim and Arab world cannot but feel offended when the media flashes headlines like "Is Islam a religion of Peace?" or "Is Islam the underlying cause of terrorism?"

The degree of misunderstanding is still dangerously high despite the genuine effort exerted by many to redress the misconceptions of the Arab world and Islam that seem rampant in the West. In fact, many people in the West still believe that the "war against terrorism is a war against Islam."

The issue of how to face terrorism is also widely discussed and debated in the Arab world. These issues are complex and manifold. In 1998, The Arab League launched the Arab Anti-Terrorism Initiative, which includes various objectives and mechanisms to combat terrorism.

Furthermore, the Arab world also recognizes that the issue of human rights is no less crucial to both security and peace. In 1994, the League of Arab States adopted the Arab Charter on Human Rights, which was revised and modified with a view to its modernization at the Arab Summit in Tunisia in March 2004.

Needless to say, the most vulnerable groups that are effected by the absence of peace and security are women and children. We in the Arab world aspire to sparing our women and children the scourges of war, armed conflict and discrimination. The Arab League launched a number of initiatives to make these aspirations a reality. Before the Convention of the Rights of the Child was issued, the League acknowledged the importance of children's rights and adopted in 1983 the Arab Charter on the Rights of the Child and in March 2001, the Arab Summit approved the Arab Framework on the Rights of the Child. The implementation of the first Arab Action Plan on Childhood commenced in 1992 and the second action plan for the period 2004–2015 was adopted by the Arab Summit in Tunisia in 2004.

These two action plans address various aspects that aim to ensure the ability of the Arab world to nurture and care for its children and youth, and to provide health, educational and social services and all forms of protection to them.

In addition to addressing these issues, the Arab world set in motion the wheel of reform, modernization and development across the region. The Arab Summit in Tunis in 2004 adopted a crucial document addressing reform, modernization and change in the Arab World. This document addresses a number of vital issues: democracy, human rights, empowerment of women, transparency and accountability as well as efforts to achieve social and economic development including the modernization of education in the Arab world.

Hundreds of projects are being implemented in each and every Arab country to achieve these objectives. These projects cover almost every aspect of life. They range from projects that aim at consolidating democratic practices, enlarging participation in political and public life, fostering the role of the civil society, widening women's participation in the political, economic, social, cultural and educational fields and reinforcing their rights and status in society.

Another important fundamental issue to the achievement of peace is that of disarmament. Fostering a culture of peace cannot be achieved without addressing the issue of the proliferation of conventional and non-conventional weapons in the region. Since 1974 the Arab world has been calling for the establishment of a zone free from all weapons of mass destruction in the Middle East. However, genuine efforts to realize this objective are yet to bear results. An important initiative that the Arab League undertook is establishing a technical committee to draw up a draft treaty for making the Middle East a zone free of all weapons of mass destruction, with the hope that one day there will be enough will and determination for its implementation.

The challenge facing all of us today is not only through enhancing our dialogue, but also by acting so that this dialogue becomes an instrument of change and transformation, a road to peace and tolerance, and a vehicle for diversity and pluralism.

Indeed, the culture of peace provides an alternative to the escalating cycle of violence in the world of today. Our shared values must inspire us towards achieving a world of peace, tolerance and understanding. Instead of enemy images, we need to foster understanding, tolerance and solidarity. Instead of armaments, the international community needs to genuinely work for universal and verifiable disarmament. Instead of totalitarianism, we must allow for the evolution of democracy and universal participation.

Dialogue should be the alternative to intolerance. Upholding the rule of law is indispensable to the achievement of peace but this can not be achieved if it is not a process which involves all our societies; nor can it be achieved without the genuine efforts of the international community.

ORGANIZATION OF AMERICAN STATES

ORGANIZATION OF AMERICAN STATES

Establishment

In 1948, twenty-one nations of the Hemisphere signed the OAS Charter, affirming their commitment to common goals and their respect for each nation's sovereignty.

But the idea of inter-American cooperation dates back much further. In the 1820s, Simón Bolívar envisioned a region "united in heart." In 1890, nations of the region formed the Commercial Bureau of American Republics, which evolved into the Pan American Union and later into the Organization of American States (OAS). Since 1948, the OAS has expanded to include the nations of the English-speaking Caribbean and Canada, giving the OAS a broader perspective that encompasses the entire Hemisphere.

The transition from the Pan American Union to the OAS was smooth.

The Organization of American States is comprised of 35 Member States.

The OAS is headquartered in Washington, D. C., USA.

Executive Head

H. E. Mr. José Miguel Insulza, Secretary-General of the OAS

Objectives

The OAS brings together the countries of the Western Hemisphere to strengthen cooperation and advance common interests. It is the region's premier forum for multi-lateral dialogue and concerted action.

At the core of the OAS mission is an unequivocal commitment to democracy, as expressed in the Inter-American Democratic Charter:

"The peoples of the Americas have a right to democracy and their governments have an obligation to promote and defend it." Building on this foundation, the OAS works to promote good governance, strengthen human rights, foster peace and security, expand trade, and address the complex problems caused by poverty, drugs and corruption. Through decisions made by its political bodies and programs carried out by its General Secretariat, the OAS promotes greater inter-American cooperation and understanding. The OAS plays a key role in strengthening democratic institutions and practices in the countries of the Americas. Guided by the principles of the Democratic Charter, the OAS also supports efforts to decentralize governments, modernize political parties, strengthen national legislatures, and consolidate democratic values and culture. It also works to promote a greater role for civil society in decision-making.

Contact Information

Organization of American States

17th Street & Constitution Ave., N. W.
Washington, D. C. 20006
USA

Telephone: + 1 202 458 3000
Telefax: + 1 202 458 6250

Internet: **http://www.oas.org**

Strengthening Peace and Democracy in the Americas:
The Role of the Organization of American States

Betilde V. Muñoz-Pogossian, Office for the Prevention and Resolution of Conflicts, OAS Department of Democratic and Political Affairs

"Recent experience has demonstrated that regional organizations can be a vital part of the multilateral system. Their efforts need not contradict United Nations efforts, nor do they absolve the United Nations (UN) of its primary responsibilities for peace and security."[1]

The international community has recently engaged in a process to underscore the importance and effectiveness of regional organizations, such as the Organization of American States (OAS), in the promotion and maintenance of international peace and security. Two examples are worth exploring. One includes the consultative process started in 1998 by the UN to discuss mechanisms to improve cooperation in the area of peacebuilding and conflict prevention between the UN system and regional organizations. This process has resulted in a shared vision by the international community about the need to strengthen conflict prevention and peacebuilding capacities of regional organizations in order to promote and maintain peace in the world.

A more recent realization of the key role of regional organizations in peacebuilding emerges from the UN High-level Panel on Threats, Challenges and Change (2004).[2] In the report, the High-level Panel sets out a bold, new vision of collective security for the 21st century emphasizing that in today's world, "a threat to one is a threat to all." While highlighting the importance of working collaboratively to address these threats and challenges to peace in the world, the High-level Panel recognizes that regional organizations can be a vital part of the multilateral system. The Report indicates how important it is to organize regional action within the framework and purposes of the UN, and to ensure that this institution and any regional organization with which it works do so in a more integrated fashion. This requires greater consultation and cooperation between the UN and regional organizations through meetings of the heads of the organizations, more frequent exchange of information and early warning, co-training of civilian and military human resources, and exchange of personnel within peace operations, among other initiatives.

Efforts like the UN consultation process and the recommendations, emerging from the UN High-level Panel, to give greater importance to regional organizations confirm the realization that these institutions have a comparative advantage to prepare and implement preventive actions to address threats to peace in their regions. In the words of UN Secretary-General Kofi Annan, "… regional organizations can contribute to conflict prevention in a number of specific ways. Such organizations build trust among States through the frequency of interaction, and have a greater grasp of the historical background of a conflict. Because of their proximity, regional organizations (can) provide a local forum for efforts to decrease tensions and promote and facilitate a comprehensive regional approach to cross-border issues."[3]

This article presents the work of such a regional organization, the OAS, in building a culture of peace and democracy in the Americas. It shows the efforts being made by the OAS towards the creation of a more peaceful, secure and prosperous environment in the Western Hemisphere, and discusses the shift in regional approaches to security in the region. The article also highlights the role of the OAS in the development of structural and practical models for addressing threats to peace and democracy within the Hemisphere, focusing on the importance of democratic governance and conflict resolution mechanisms.

A New Environment:
Redefining Challenges to Peace and Security in the Americas

The traditional concern of interstate conflict between American states has become less urgent nowadays. With the exception of a few territorial and border disputes, the Americas are considered to be one of the most secure and peaceful regions in the world. In fact, since the early 1990s, from the 12 existing interstate disputes within the Americas, only the case of the border dispute between Peru and Ecuador in 1995 escalated into armed struggle. The few remaining territorial disputes are currently being resolved through negotiation and other peaceful conflict resolution processes. In these disputes, the OAS has become a key facilitator and honorable broker of sensitive political negotiations, especially through the OAS Fund for Peace.[4] Two examples are described here, i.e. the case of the territorial dispute between Honduras and Nicaragua, and that between Guatemala and Belize.

In 1999, tensions emerged between Honduras and Nicaragua over their unsettled maritime boundaries in the Caribbean Sea. To prevent an escalation of this tension,

Organization of American States

both countries requested the help of the OAS, and thus the OAS Permanent Council approved a resolution calling for the Secretary General to nominate a Special Envoy to "evaluate the situation, facilitate dialogue, and formulate recommendations aimed at easing tensions and preventing acts that could affect peace in the Hemisphere." A Special Envoy was appointed to assist the countries, and over a period of three months, Honduras and Nicaragua reached three agreements that instituted a set of confidence-building measures as well as an interim mechanism to ensure peaceful relations. The agreements served to contain an escalation of the dispute while the substance of their boundary dispute was decided by the International Court of Justice. A March 2000 agreement between the parties spelled out specific measures to maintain communications between the two countries' armed forces, to restrict military activities along the border, and to conduct joint patrols in the Caribbean Sea as well as independent patrols over the respective jurisdictional waters in the Gulf of Fonseca.[5]

With the support of the OAS, Honduras and Nicaragua signed a technical agreement the following year for observation and verification by third parties on their compliance with the measures that had been previously agreed. In June 2001, both countries signed an agreement at the OAS detailing the Civilian Verification Mission. The Honduras-Nicaragua dispute resolution process ended in December 2001 when this mission's final report was presented.

The OAS Fund for Peace has also been critical in facilitating the successful resolution of the territorial dispute between Guatemala and Belize. The OAS was invited to serve as a Witness of Honor in the bilateral meetings between the two countries. Various technical and ministerial meetings took place at OAS Headquarters and the countries agreed on a framework for negotiation on July 20, 2000. A Panel of Facilitators was installed to help guide the negotiation process in August 2000. Belize and Guatemala also established a so-called Adjacency Zone in the border and created a Mixed Commission to promote good relations among the communities in the area. In September 2002, the Panel of Facilitators presented to the Governments a document with a set of proposals for the just, equitable and permanent solution to their territorial differendum, with the understanding that the Proposals were to be adopted or rejected, by both countries, by a referendum.

An agreement was signed on February 7, 2003 by the Foreign Ministers of Belize and Guatemala, along with the Secretary General and Assistant Secretary General of the OAS to establish a Transition Process and a series of confidence-building measures between the two countries. This agreement sets up a mechanism to manage the Belize-Guatemala relationship following the conclusion of the Facilitation Process, and following the postponement of the national referendums to adopt or reject the proposals of the Mixed Commission. This recent agreement outlines a framework with the responsibilities of the Parties and also assigns responsibilities to the OAS General Secretariat, and to the international community through the establishment of a "Group of Friends" to support the peaceful resolution of the Belize-Guatemala territorial differendum. The consideration of these proposals by the people of both countries through a referendum has not yet taken place and remains one of the pending issues in the Belizean and Guatemalan political agendas.

The probability of the emergence of interstate conflict may decrease as countries of the region continue to work towards the creation of the necessary conditions to prevent such situations from developing into ones in which one state takes violent action against another. The region has engaged in a process of securing ties of friendship, trust and cooperation. New threats are now emerging from within states.

Indeed, the regional context shows that intrastate conflicts are becoming more common than interstate conflicts, representing almost 90 % of the total number of world conflicts. Internal tensions and conflicts have been a recurrent phenomenon in Latin America. Between 1990 and 2005, there have been various coups d'état; at least 12 presidential destitutions/resignations[6]; frequent cases of internal military tensions; and one ongoing internal conflict (Colombia), not to mention multiple strikes, road-blocks, and social mobilizations.

Thus, the "old" hemispheric system relied on legal frameworks that dealt with traditional threats to peace and security in the context of interstate conflict. The Rio Treaty – TIAR – (1947), Bogota Pact (1948), and the Treaty of Tlatelolco for the non-proliferation of weapons of mass destruction in the Americas (1967) are examples. The current institutional framework, however, now includes a diverse range of hemispheric legal instruments, treaties, ad hoc mechanisms for the resolution of conflict, and confidence-building measures that deal with both traditional and non-traditional concerns.

Institutional Mandates:
The Role of the OAS in building a Culture of Peace in the Americas

Democracy, peace and security have been at the heart of OAS institutional mandates. In light of the changing environment in which traditional threats are not the norm but intrastate conflict takes on great significance, the OAS' response through successive mandates, summit agreements, and most recently, the adoption of the Inter-American Democratic Charter (IADC) have highlighted the importance of adapting institutional initiatives to respond to the new needs and demands of its member states.

For one, preventive diplomacy and crisis management are at the heart of the OAS Charter and other regional instruments. Like that of the UN, the OAS Charter is dedicated primarily to disputes at the interstate level. The OAS Charter calls on member states to "prevent possible causes of difficulties," to "ensure the pacific settlement of disputes that may arise among the Member States," and to "strengthen the peace and security of the continent".[4]

In the realm of peace, democracy, and development, OAS instruments repeatedly make a crucial link. In the OAS Charter's preamble, as well as in the Santiago Declaration of 1991, representative democracy is described as "an indispensable condition for the stability, peace and development of the region". Other instruments continue to stress the importance of promoting democracy and peace in the Americas, especially in terms of preventing the emergence of conflict. The General Assembly Declaration of Managua for the Promotion of Democracy and Development[7] explicitly states that "the Organization's mission is not restricted to the defense of democracy where its values and fundamental principles have collapsed" and calls on the member states "to undertake creative and constant work towards the consolidation of democracy as well as maintain ongoing efforts to prevent and anticipate the causes of problems that work against democratic governance."

More recently, the goal of promoting democracy and peace in the Hemisphere, and strengthening governance motivated the member states of the OAS to adopt the Inter-American Democratic Charter, signed on September 11, 2001 in Lima, Peru. This document works to expand, organize, and strengthen existing legal instruments, furthering the development, consolidation, promotion, and defense of democracy in the region. Furthermore, the IADC widens the scope of OAS activities to confront the growing crisis of democracy member states currently face. Specifically, the

IADC facilitates the possibility of early, rapid and preventive response to crisis situations in the member states.

The Role of the OAS in Prevention and Resolution of Intrastate Conflicts

Over the past few years, the OAS has worked towards the development of actions and institutional capacity for dealing with the internal problems of member states. This support comes through new agreements, direct assistance for dialogue processes (including special ad hoc missions), and local capacity building measures, which focus on indirect support to assist member states constructively manage conflict and consensus building.

In most of Central and South America, and some parts of the Caribbean, the key factor fueling conflict has been the emergence of demands for change coming from society. Lack of flexibility and inclusiveness in certain systems of government has limited these governments' ability to effectively respond to demands for equity, economic advancement, participation and power sharing. Elections and representative democracy are not sufficient for initiating and sustaining the changes needed to achieve truly stable, prosperous and peaceful societies in the Western Hemisphere. The lack of trained professionals in conflict prevention and resolution, the design of dialogue processes, third party facilitation and consensus building skills has resulted in numerous and repeated "failed attempts" at building government-civil society bridges, calling into question the value or viability of dialogue as an effective tool for managing and resolving conflict.

As new spaces for citizen participation in the public policy arena are created, member states increasingly request OAS assistance in developing and implementing inclusive approaches and processes for dealing with intrastate conflict. Through its participation in various peace-building missions throughout the Americas[8], the OAS has acquired technical and political expertise working with member states in generating minimum conditions for national dialogue, institutionalizing mechanisms for conflict management, and strengthening national and sub-regional capacities in consensus building and negotiation. As the Hemisphere's leading political forum and in light of this ample field experience, the OAS is uniquely positioned to take the lead in democracy promotion and conflict resolution efforts in the Americas. Moreover, as events in other parts of the world absorb the attention of many multilateral organizations, there is an ideal space for the Organization to assume a prominent role in furthering innovative and peaceful solutions to the national and regional problems confronting the region's democracies.

The current challenge posed to the OAS is how to consolidate these types of mechanisms and institutional forms of support toward the completion of these important tasks. It is of crucial importance to develop an evaluation system and systematization of lessons learned from which the expertise of the OAS could be enriched and shared. To achieve this, former Secretary General of the OAS, Cesar Gaviria, created a small office within the Secretariat with the task of supporting these types of missions by the Offices of the Secretary and Assistant Secretary General. Later in 2004 in a system-wide reorganization process within the Secretariat, the Office for the Prevention and Resolution of Conflict (OPRC) absorbed this small office and was institutionalized within the new Department of Democratic and Political Affairs with the task of providing technical assistance and advisory services to member states in the development and institutionalization of national capacity to conduct political dialogue processes and prevent and resolve intrastate conflicts.

The Department of Democratic and Political Affairs (DDPA) and its Office for the Prevention and Resolution of Conflicts (OPRC)

The structure and operations of the OAS in the field of conflict prevention and resolution were revamped in 2004 to establish a focal point for early warning and conflict prevention in the Department of Democratic and Political Affairs. The goal of the OPRC is to provide solid, clear and strategic political analysis of complex situations which may lead to the eruption of violent interstate and intrastate conflict in the Americas.

Formally established through Executive Order No. 05-03 Corr. 1, the OPRC provides support and technical assistance to create and strengthen the national institutional capacity of member states to efficiently and successfully manage internal conflicts. This reflects the work of the Department as a whole as it reinforces institutional democracy within countries of the Hemisphere. The task currently undertaken by the DDPA and the OPRC is to provide the means by which societies can reach at least a minimal level of consensus necessary within public political debate in order to preserve democratic institutions and principles, while simultaneously fostering an environment to prevent the violent eruption of crisis or latent conflict, as well as peacefully resolve national disputes.

This assistance is provided to member states at the national, regional, or sub-regional levels, and includes:
– Assistance to member states in the design and integration into practice of integral systems for the promotion of dialogue, prevention, and resolution of conflicts;
– Specialized capacity building;
– Support to the sustained process of exchange of experiences and best practices among member states;
– Indirect facilitation in support of dialogue processes and/or negotiation, with emphasis on process-oriented assistance (technical assistance for negotiations, conciliation, or the establishment of a "pre-dialogue" environment).

The last point stresses the "process" orientation of assistance, and not thematic and substantive advice. One of the most successful experiences of the OAS has been the Program "Culture of Dialogue: Development of Resources for Peacebuilding in Guatemala, OAS/PROPAZ". This OAS Program aimed to contribute to the creation of conditions and processes that enable the transition from confrontation towards a "culture of dialogue" in Guatemala. The Program provided training in communication and conflict resolution skills, negotiation, mediation and conciliation to a variety of Guatemalan actors working at different levels of society. The Program's mission was to support the establishment of an infrastructure for peacebuilding, democratization and reconciliation in Guatemala and explicitly recognized that these processes were inter-related. Recently, the OAS transferred the mandates, vision and methodologies of the PROPAZ Program to the Guatemalan society with the establishment of the ProPaz Foundation. With this, the OAS accomplished one of the Program's main objectives: to leave installed capacity in Guatemala to continue supporting the country's peace and political dialogue processes and the strengthening of democracy.

At the national level, the OPRC is developing a project for the design and implementation of a conflict prevention and resolution system in Bolivia. The OPRC Program in Bolivia focuses on socio-political conflict(s) that affect local or national governance and typically involve government and civil society actors and institutions. Attention is given to the relational and substantive aspects of conflict. Process and program interventions aim at fostering systemic change by developing alternative patterns of behavior and new social dynamics based on cooperation, inclusion and shared responsibility rather than confrontation and exclusion. This Program adopts a multi-sectoral approach to dialogue and conflict resolution, and explicitly includes steps to generate conditions to enable parties in conflict to engage constructively in joint analysis and resolution of socio-political conflict(s) that affect their democracy.

In Colombia, the OAS Mission to Support the Peace Process (MAPP/OAS) was formally established in February 2004 with the adoption of Permanent Council Resolution 859. The Mission has worked hand in hand with the Colombian Government and people in their efforts to achieve a firm and long-long lasting peace in that country. The MAPP focuses its efforts along three thematic lines: 1) verification of the ceasefire and cessation of hostilities, disarmament, demobilization, and reintegration, 2) verification of the weapons that are surrendered by the demobilized combatants and 3) support for local initiatives in conflict zones, by promoting confidence-building measures and reconciliation. The Mission has been present at the demobilization of more than 4,800 members of the Autodefensas Unidas de Colombia (AUC) in different regions of the country. Presently, the MAPP is engaged in perhaps the most important aspect of the current peace process: the accompaniment of the reincorporation of the demobilized fighters into civilian society.

At the sub-regional level, the OPRC is working on the implementation of the Central American Program for the Strengthening of Democratic Dialogue (PCA). This initiative strives for the promotion of multi-sectoral dialogue at the sub-regional level on critical issues of common interest, (e.g. crime prevention and land reform), among Central American nations. Over a three-year period, this Program aims to develop a sub-regional infrastructure to facilitate processes and establishing conflict management mechanisms between national, regional and hemispheric counterparts working in the area of consensus building, dialogue and governance in Central America.

Moreover, this initiative strives to strengthen the institutional capacity of government agencies and civil society organizations engaged in socio-political dialogue. Finally, through this initiative, the OPRC hopes to provide opportunities for an exchange of experiences and best practices in capacity building and training in conflict resolution, and allow for feedback, and systematization among the Central American countries.

With the establishment of an Office within the structure of the DADP, the OAS is consolidating a more strategic role in the democratization processes underway in the

Americas and is becoming a reference point of assistance to member states in developing mechanisms that would help regulate and manage potential violent conflict.

Institutionalizing Dialogue in the Americas

A mechanism that has proved successful in dealing and preventing conflict in several situations is the implementation of dialogue processes. In the last few years, there has been greater awareness about the importance of the institutionalization of these mechanisms not only as a means to manage or even solve existing conflicts, but also as a longer term system of public policy formulation. Through the 2003 General Assembly Resolution on the Promotion and Strengthening of Democracy: Follow-up to the Inter-American Democratic Charter[9], the member states instructed the Permanent Council to "continue to promote the exchange of experiences and best practices, so as to institutionalize dialogue as a means of promoting democratic governance and resolving conflicts." They also asked the General Secretariat to "continue developing mechanisms for dialogue and instruments for the prevention and resolution of conflicts, so as to support the member states in their interactions with various political and social actors."

Dialogue is considered by the OPRC as an instrument to maintain peace in the countries of the Hemisphere and is "seen as part of a longer-term strategy that remains unaffected by time sensitive crises. Dialogue tends to lead to the kinds of agreements and relationships between actors that are likely to survive changes in administrations and become national policies".[10]

The OPRC has the "know-how" and experience to help member states build capacities for conflict prevention and resolution, and dialogue design within their governmental structures. One of the main responsibilities of the OPRC is to promote government and civil society collaboration through consensus building and participatory mechanisms as a tool for strengthening democratic governance and public policy formulation[11]. In this sense, the OPRC plans to continue implementing programs that "would seek to promote the exchange of experiences and policy recommendations for improving government-civil society relations, enhancing political dialogue and increasing citizen participation in the formulation of public policy as tools for strengthening democratic governance".[12]

At the global level, efforts to foster and develop new relationships with other regional and intergovernmental organizations will prove beneficial as the OAS continues to manage the arduous task of combating new transnational and regional threats to security. Information sharing among the various agencies and organizations involved in conflict prevention and resolution can contribute to gathering and recording a set of best practices to confront the threats to peace, democracy and development in the Americas. In a multilateral world where interstate and intrastate conflicts as well as transnational threats affect us all, it is crucial to work collaboratively to address them and promote a culture of peace in the world.

1   Report of the UN Secretary General's High-level Panel on Threats, Challenges and Change (2004).

2   In his address to the General Assembly in September 2003, United Nations Secretary-General Kofi Annan warned UN member states that the United Nations needed to rise to the challenge of meeting new threats or it could risk erosion in the face of mounting discord between States and unilateral action by them. He then created the High-level Panel on Threats, Challenges and Change to generate new ideas about the kinds of policies and institutions required for the UN to be effective in the 21st century.

3   UN Secretary General's 2001 Report on the Prevention of Armed Conflict.

4   The Fund for Peace (or Fund for Peace: Peaceful Resolution of Territorial Disputes) was formally established through Resolution AG/RES. 1756 (XXX-O/00) by the Foreign Ministers of the Hemisphere meeting at the OAS' General Assembly in Windsor, Canada in June 2000, as a mechanism to provide financial resources to member states of the Organization that so request, in order to assist them with defraying the costs of proceedings previously agreed by the Parties for the peaceful resolution of territorial disputes.

5   Soto, Yadira. 2004. "The Role of the Organization of American States in Conflict Prevention" In Schnabel & Carment (ed). 2004. Conflict Prevention: From Rhetoric to Reality. Lexington Books.

6   Ecuador (2000); Argentina (2001); Venezuela (2002); Bolivia (2003); Ecuador (2005), among others.

7   Document (GA/DEC. 4 (XXIII-O/93).

8   The OAS builds on the technical and political expertise acquired from a variety of OAS specialized peacebuilding missions and recent conflict mediation experiences in Peru, Haiti, Colombia, Nicaragua, and Guatemala.

9   Document AG/RES. 1957 (XXXIII-O/03).

10 Dialogue and Governance in Latin America, OPRC's Working Papers Series.

11 OAS, General Secretariat, Executive Order No. 05–03, Annex C.

12 OPRC 2005 Work Plan.

ORGANIZATION OF
THE ISLAMIC CONFERENCE

ORGANIZATION OF THE ISLAMIC CONFERENCE

Establishment

The Organization of the Islamic Conference (OIC) is an intergovernmental organization grouping 57 States. These States decided to pool their resources together, combine their efforts and speak with one voice to safeguard the interest and ensure the progress and well-being of their peoples and those of other Muslims in the world over.

The Organization of The Islamic Conference was established in Rabat, Morocco, on 12 Rajab 1389H (25 September 1969) during the first meeting of the leaders of the Islamic world.

Six months after that historical meeting, i. e. in Muharram 1390H (March 1970), the First Islamic Conference of Ministers of Foreign Affairs held in Jeddah, Saudi Arabia, set up a permanent General Secretariat, to ensure a liaison among Member States and charged it to coordinate their action. The Conference decided to establish the OIC Headquarters in Jeddah. Two and a half years after Rabat, in Muharram 1392H (February 1972), the Islamic Conference of Foreign Ministers, meeting in its Third Session, adopted the Charter of the Organization, whose purpose is to strengthen solidarity and cooperation among Islamic States in the political, economic, cultural, scientific and social fields.

Executive Head

H. E. Prof. Ekmeleddin Ihsanoglu, Secretary-General of the OIC

Objectives

The Organization of The Islamic Conference aims to:

– **Strengthen:** Islamic solidarity among Member States; Cooperation in the political, economic, social, cultural and scientific fields; The struggle of all Muslim people to safeguard their dignity, independence and national rights.

– **Coordinate action to:** Safeguard the Holy Places; Support the struggle of the Palestinian people and assist them in recovering their rights and liberating their occupied territories.

– **Work to:** Eliminate racial discrimination and all forms of colonialism; Create a favorable atmosphere for the promotion of cooperation and understanding between Member States and other countries.

Contact Information

Organization of The Islamic Conference

P. O. Box 178
Jeddah 21411
Saudi Arabia

Telephone: + 966 2 6900001
Fax: + 966 2 2751953

Internet: **http://www.oic-oci.org**

The Organization of The Islamic Conference:
An Organization Striving to Promote Cooperation and Understanding among its 57 Member States as well as with the International Community

H. E. Prof. Ekmeleddin Ihsanoglu, Secretary-General of the OIC

The cardinal objective of the Organization of Islamic Conference (OIC)'s Charter of promoting cooperation and understanding among member states and with the international community, places the Organization at a unique position in multilateral efforts to seek common grounds both between and within various civilizations in order to collectively confront the unprecedented contemporary global challenges. The OIC, accordingly, is playing a pivotal role in bridging the ever-increasing gulf of misunderstanding between Islam and the West.

The OIC Charter not only expresses the resolve of its member states to preserve their spiritual, ethical, social and economic values, but also reaffirms their commitment to the UN Charter and Fundamental Human Rights. The aims and objectives of the OIC have been defined, inter alia, as solidarity and consolidation of cooperation among its member states in the political, economic, social, cultural, scientific and other vital fields as well as their contribution towards the establishment and maintenance of international peace and security.

With 57-member states representing more than one-fifth of humanity, the OIC is not only the second largest international organization after the United Nations, but also encompasses a wide geographical span which stretches from Indonesia in the East to Guyana in the West. In economic terms, all OIC member states are developing countries and, in political terms, they all belong to the Third World.

In a relatively short span of time since its establishment in Rabat in September 1969, the OIC has come to be internationally recognized and respected. The organization continues to play an important role in the political, economic, social, cultural, scientific and technical fields and has strived to forge unity and solidarity amongst its member states. It has evolved appropriate collective policy decisions and initiatives and sought to promote political unity, socio-economic progress and cultural renaissance of its member states. It has also served as the spokesman of its member states in various international and regional forums so as to effectively project their point of view on all issues of common concern. The activities of the Organization have also gradually expanded to include many areas of cooperation, which are being implemented through a network of OIC Specialized Agencies, Institutions and Centres.

Structurally, the OIC comprises the following three main organs, as defined in its Charter:

i. **Conference of Heads of State and Governments:** Being the highest policy-making body of the organization, these Summit Conferences are held every three years to periodically review the entire spectrum of conditions within its member states as well as the international situation and to elaborate strategies and objectives. The last 10th Summit Conference was held in Putrajaya, Malaysia in October 2003.

ii. **Conference of Foreign Ministers:** During its annual meetings, significant international developments are deliberated upon and collective positions on global political and economic issues are evolved. The last 31st Conference of Foreign Ministers was held in Istanbul, Turkey in June 2004.

iii. **The OIC General Secretariat:** Based in Jeddah, it is headed by the Secretary General and is responsible for ensuring the follow-up and implementation of the decisions adopted by the Summit and Ministerial Conferences. It also coordinates the activities of OIC's affiliated institutions as well as its specialized and subsidiary organs, which have been established to promote cooperation in wide-ranging diverse economic, socio-cultural, scientific and technological fields. OIC's first democratically elected Secretary General, H. E. Professor Ekmeleddin Ihsanoglu, assumed office for a four year term on January 1st, 2005.

The institutional structure of the OIC system has also gradually expanded itself and presently comprises the following various functional bodies:

i. **Specialized Committees:** These include the "OIC Ministerial Committees" for Palestine, Afghanistan; Solidarity with the Peoples of the Sahel (CILSS) and Muslims in Southern Philippines as well as the "OIC Contact Groups" for Bosnia-Herzegovina; Jammu and Kashmir; Sierra Leone; Somalia and Reform of the UN and its Security Council.

ii. **Special Committees & Organs:** These include the Al-Quds Committee and the "three Standing Committees" for Information and Cultural Affairs (COMIAC); Economic & Commercial Cooperation (COMCEC) and Scientific and Technological Cooperation (COMSTECH). In addition there are "four Preparatory Meetings' Committees" i.e. the Senior Officials Meeting (SOM); the Islamic Commission for Economic, Cultural and Social Affairs (ICECS); the Financial Control Organ (FCO), and the Permanent Finance Committee (PFC).

iii. **Affiliated Institutions:** These include the Islamic Chamber of Commerce and Industry; the Organization of Islamic Capitals; the Sports Federation of Islamic Solidarity Games; the Islamic Committee of the International Crescent; the Islamic Ship-owners Association; the World Federation of International Arab-Islamic Schools and the International Association of Islamic Banks.

iv. **Independent Universities:** These include the International Islamic University in Malaysia as well as in Bangladesh.

v. **Specialized Organs:** These include the Islamic Development Bank (IDB); the Islamic Educational, Scientific and Cultural Organization (ISESCO); the International Islamic News Agency (IINA) and the Islamic States Broadcasting Organization (ISBO).

vi. **Subsidiary Organs:** These include the Statistical, Economic and Social Research and Training Centre (SESTRIC); the Research Centre for Islamic History, Arts and Culture (IRCICA); the Islamic University of Technology; the Islamic Centre for Development of Trade (ICDT) and the Islamic Fiqh Academy.

vii. **OIC External Offices:** These include the two OIC Permanent Observer Missions to the United Nations in New York and Geneva as well as the OIC Office for Afghanistan.

viii. **Contribution Organs:** These include the Permanent Council of the Islamic Solidarity Fund (ISF) and its Waqf; the Al-Quds Fund & its Waqf; the three OIC Trust Funds to assist the reconstruction efforts in Afghanistan, Bosnia-Herzegovina and Sierra Leone as well as the Islamic Universities of Niger and Uganda.

In the political field, the OIC has continued to focus special attention upon and review significant developments in the Middle East, particularly those concerning the Palestinian issue. While reiterating its support for all international efforts to peacefully resolve the issue, the OIC has continued to extend its full support to the inalienable rights of the Palestinian people and has called for a comprehensive, peaceful, just and durable solution to the Palestinian issue.

An OIC Ministerial delegation held useful meetings with representatives of all the Quartet members in their respective headquarters in the second half of 2004 and urged them to intensify their efforts to achieve a just and comprehensive peace in the Middle East within a specified time-frame. Since a number of its member states have emerged from the yoke of colonialism, the OIC has also continued to extend its full solidarity with and supported national liberation movements and peoples struggling against colonialism, racial discrimination and apartheid.

The OIC has also continued to provide a framework for a regular, systematic and institutionalized review of significant international political developments by its member states. This review, which has resulted in the evolution of numerous collective policy decisions and initiatives, has interalia focused on the situation in Afghanistan; Azerbaijan; Cyprus; Iraq; Jammu and Kashmir; the peace process between India and Pakistan; Somalia and Sudan as well as reform of the UN Security Council and important disarmament issues.

Ever since his assumption of office, the new OIC Secretary General, Professor Ekmeleddin Ihsanoglu, has continued to exchange views on the situation in Iraq during all his meetings with the leaders of OIC member states. Likewise, the General Secretariat is closely following the developments and the rapidly evolving situation in Iraq. The OIC Secretary General actively participated in both the International Conference on Iraq in Sharm el-Sheikh in November 2004 and the 8th meeting of the Neighbouring Countries of Iraq in Istanbul in April 2005. The OIC Secretary General has been invited to an International Conference on Iraq in Brussels on 22 June 2005. It would be worthwhile to mention that apart from the UN, the OIC is the only other organization in which Iraq and all its neighbouring countries are its members.

Upon the request of the UN Secretary General and the Government of Sudan, two OIC missions visited Darfur in June 2004 and recently again in May 2005. In addition, upon the request of the concerned counties, the OIC sent its observers to monitor the elections in Chechnya and Afghanistan during 2004.

A significant illustration of OIC's collaboration with the UN and its specialized agencies is the ongoing joint preparations with the UNHCR for a proposed OIC Ministerial Conference on Refugees in the Muslim World in the second half of 2005.

The OIC has also supported President Musharraf of Pakistan's timely initiative of a two-pronged strategy of "Enlightened Moderation" in order to build international peace and harmony, promote moderation, oppose extremism and ensure justice. The strategy entails, on the one hand, internal reform and renewal, eschewing extremism and confrontation as well as socio-economic development amongst Muslim countries and, on the other hand, by simultaneous efforts by the West to help resolve political disputes affecting Muslim peoples, by rejecting attempts to equate Islam with terrorism and by assisting the Muslim World in their socio-economic development. An OIC Commission of Eminent Persons has recently finalized its recommendations in this regard.

The OIC, like the international community, has also continued to focus its attention on the scourge of international terrorism. The organization's involvement with this issue could be gauged from the fact that it organized an international seminar on the "Phenomenon of Terrorism in the Contemporary World and its Impact on Individual Security, Political Stability and International Peace" in Geneva as far back as June 1987.

All OIC Summit and Ministerial Conferences have continued to strongly condemn terrorism in all its forms and manifestations and have expressed sympathy and support for those countries which have become victims of such shameful acts. The OIC has, however, continued to reiterate that terrorism should be clearly distinguished from peoples' struggle to achieve their inalienable right to self-determination. The OIC has also supported efforts to convene an International Conference, under the auspices of the UN, to comprehensively define terrorism. It has also supported efforts to establish an OIC Code of Conduct on Combating International Terrorism. The OIC has successively adopted resolutions to strengthen Islamic solidarity in combating terrorism and urged its member states to accede to as well as strictly implement the provisions of the relevant 13 UN Conventions in this regard.

In the aftermath of the 9/11 tragedy, an extraordinary OIC Ministerial Conference was held in Doha, Qatar in October 2001. An OIC Convention on Combating International Terrorism entered into force in November 2002.

In April 2002, an Extraordinary Ministerial Meeting on Terrorism was held in Kuala Lumpur. As a result of this meeting, an OIC Ministerial Committee on Terrorism was established under the chairmanship of Malaysia. The OIC actively participated in the Counter-Terrorism International Conference in Riyadh in February 2005 as well as in other international seminars on terrorism organized by the UN and its specialized bodies, particularly the CTC, as well as other international and regional organizations.

Pursuant to the resolutions adopted by its successive Summit and Ministerial Conferences, the OIC has also continued to attach special interest to the issue of Muslim minorities in non-member states. The OIC Secretariat has established direct contacts, collected information and reports relating to the conditions of Muslim minorities in non-member states and convened conferences and symposia in these states. The objectives of these contacts has been to ascertain the conditions of these Muslim minorities, identification of their problems and attempt to find appropriate solutions in cooperation with the Governments of these non-OIC states. Accordingly, in close cooperation with the Governments of Philippines, Thailand and the Russian Federation, respectively, the OIC is playing a vital role in pursuing a peaceful settlement of the conflicts in Southern Philippines, Southern Thailand and Chechnya.

In close collaboration with the respective Governments, the voluntary OIC Trust Funds for Afghanistan, Bosnia-Herzegovina and Sierra Leone, continue to undertake numerous projects for the reconstruction and rehabilitation of these war-stricken countries.

As an illustration of its support for global humanitarian efforts, the OIC promptly established an OIC Coalition to Rescue Child Victims of the tragic Tsumami disaster in South East Asia. So far, over 30,000 orphans and child victims are being taken care of and being provided assistance by this Coalition.

In the economic field, the OIC has actively participated in international deliberations relating to globalization; WTO; hunger and food security; poverty alleviation; the Highly Indebted Poor Countries Initiative (HIPC) as well as the problems confronted by LDCs. The OIC has also undertaken a number of activities under the two OIC Plans of Action to Strengthen Economic and Commercial Cooperation as well as for the Development and Promotion of Tourism among its Member States. The OIC has also concluded various agreements, which notably include the Framework Agreement on the Trade Preferential System among OIC Member States; the Agreement on Promotion, Protection & Guarantee of Investments; Statute of the Islamic Civil Aviation Council; Statute of the Islamic Telecommunication Union and the Statute of the Standards and Metrology Institute for Islamic Countries.

With the objective of strengthening economic cooperation amongst its member states, the OIC, with the initiative of Malaysia, has recently launched an intra-OIC Capacity-Building Program. Under the first phase of this Program, three pilot projects in Bangladesh, Sierra Leone and Mauritania, have been initiated and four additional projects have been identified for the second phase.

Ever since its establishment in 1975, the Islamic Development Bank has continued to play a vital role in supporting development programmes, financing trade, developing industry and infrastructure as well as in promoting technical assistance programmes in OIC Member States. IDB has also undertaken an invaluable assistance programme to improve the pathetic conditions of the people of the African Sahel as well as victims of drought and famine in Africa.

In the field of science & technology, the OIC and its affiliated institutions, like COMSTECH, ISESCO and the Islamic University of Technology, have exchanged expertise in various fields of science and technology amongst member states in order to harness them for the socio-economic development of OIC member states.

In the cultural field, the OIC has been undertaking numerous activities, which interalia includes the Cultural Strategy for the Islamic World, including Palestine and the occupied territories; the Cultural Aspects of Globalization; Promotion of Waqfs and its role in Islamic Societies; Protection of Islamic Heritage, Mosques and Holy Places; the Protection of the Muslim Child; Education & Rehabilitation of Muslim Youth; the Role of Women in the Development of Muslim Society; Combatting Narcotic Drugs; the Control of Epidemic Diseases; Environmental Protection and support for the preparation of related studies and publications. In close collaborations with its affiliated institutions like ISESCO and IRCICA, the OIC has also organized numerous international seminars and symposiums.

As a reflection of the Islam's true spirit of tolerance, peaceful coexistence, cooperation and mutual understanding with other civilizations, cultures and religions, President Khatami of Iran's proposal of Dialogue among Civilizations to the 53rd UNGA session was endorsed under Resolution 53/22 and the year 2001 designated as the "Year for Dialogue Among Civilizations".[4] There has subsequently been increased interest amongst member states and an ongoing coordination between the UN, OIC, UNESCO, ISESCO and ALESCO to establish and implement adequate cultural, educational and social programs aimed at enhancing this concept and to convene an international conference. ISESCO has prepared three editions of a White Book, organized numerous symposia and prepared scholarly studies on this subject. The OIC also welcomed the unanimous adoption of a resolution by the 58th UNGA session on the promotion of religious and cultural understanding.

The terrible tragedy of 9/11 also revealed, among other things, the vulnerability of the basic understanding among different cultures and civilizations and to erroneously identify terrorism on cultural and religious lines. Against this background, Turkey took the timely initiative of convening the first-ever OIC-EU Joint Ministerial Forum entitled "Civilization and Harmony: the Political Dimension" in Istanbul in February 2002. Unfortunately, the second meeting of this forum, which was scheduled to be held in Istanbul in October 2004, had to be cancelled at the eleventh hour. The OIC believes that this important forum, which brings together the two largest group of nations in Eurasia and Africa, can significantly contribute in reinforcing understanding and the promotion of harmony, tolerance and coherence in international relations. Another important OIC member state, Yemen, hosted an international symposium on "Human Rights and Cultures" in Sana'a in February 2004.

In close collaboration with UNICEF, the OIC has organized the First Islamic Conference on Child Care and Protection in Islam; a conference, which has taken place in Rabat in September 2005.

In the field of human rights, the OIC has continued to support efforts to defend human rights causes and espouse the noble values of Islam, which are founded on the principles of peace, tolerance, equality, good governance, social justice, accountability and the freedom of belief. The OIC has projected Islam's abhorrence and prohibition of all manifestations of discrimination, racism, corruption, disruption of public order and terrorism. With a view to signifying the importance of human rights, the OIC has adopted since 1990 a Covenant on Human Rights, which was subsequently incorporated in the OIC's Cairo Declaration on Human Rights in Islam. These documents are based not only on true Islamic values but are also inspired by the provisions of the Universal Declaration on Human Rights and other international instruments.

The OIC's ongoing comprehensive reform programme aimed at enhancing the organization's role as an effective partner at the global level has led to an increased interest on the part of the international community, including a number of regional and international organizations, to establish relations of cooperation with the OIC. The international community now increasingly recognizes OIC's position as an interlocutor with well-balanced, constructive and principled positions on global and regional issues; its abhorrence of violence and extremism as well as its persistent endeavours to institute a new world order based on justice, equality and peace.

The terrible terrorist atrocity of 9/11 jolted the foundations of the international system and triggered a profound transformation of the global geopolitical and economic landscape with unpredictable consequences. The subsequent war in Iraq under the doctrine of preemptive or preventive use of force has also been a watershed for the post-Cold War collective efforts by the international community towards conflict resolution, peacekeeping, humanitarian and nation-building as well as social and economic development. The war in Iraq, therefore, constitutes a real challenge to the concept of multilateralism.

Due to the widening of the gulf between Islam and the West, the thesis of a clash of civilizations is being taken more seriously than ever. The alarming phenomena of Islamophobia by irrational voices of hatred and bigotry in the West has exacerbated emotions against Muslims and has demonized the noble values of Islam – a religion of peace, mercy and compassion. This had created a widespread anti-western sentiment in the Islamic world and instilled a sense of alienation within the Muslim communities in the West. While extremism and militancy continue to rise within Muslim societies, a perception is spreading in the Muslim world that the West is targeting Islam and Muslims. Islam and Muslims are being equated with terrorism, extremism and intolerance. Even genuine freedom movements are being maligned as terrorism. All this is happening at a time when Islamic countries and people subsist at the margins of the global society and are gripped with fractured polity, disharmony and despair.

We are on the cusp of a new Millennium and a decisive moment in world history which calls for reflection, introspection and action. The international community must collectively strive to be the catalysts of change, not the prophets of doom. We must decide whether to flow with the currents that threaten confrontation and collapse of our civilization or muster the collective will to chart the course of history towards a peaceful, cooperative and truly global society. The international community must collectively bear the enormous responsibility to rescue the world from the vicious cycle of war and violence as well as from poverty and pestilence. We must urgently redress inequity and impoverishment which breeds despair and destruction. We must collectively construct a new global architecture of peace and prosperity for all peoples and nations.

The war against terrorism must be fought comprehensively and collectively, on a global front, with vision and understanding. It should not be allowed to erode the moral values of our societies. It must not be hijacked by those who seek to use it as an excuse to suppress other peoples. Most importantly, it must not be allowed to engender a clash of civilizations – a clash between Islam and the West.

The crisis and conflicts of the recent turbulent years have enhanced, and not diminished, the relevance of the United Nations and its concomitant multilateralism. The United Nations remains the central forum for dialogue and diplomacy and the promotion of global peace and security. For now six decades, the United Nations has been the indispensable international body for building coalitions and support, for identifying and responding to human rights violations, for international socio-economic development, for elaborating as well as enforcing international law, for advancing open trade and sound economic policies, for keeping peace and for securing the comity of nations from the threats of weapons of mass destruction and organized crime.

There has never been any doubt that the United Nations provides the ideal framework for the peaceful settlement of disputes and conflicts and for cooperation among nations. However, the objectives of the United Nations will remain unattainable without the cooperation and united action of all states as well as regional and international organizations. The United Nations must be strengthened and infused with a new spirit of collective resolve by the international community to overcome the present charged and confrontationist global environment.

It is against this perspective of international cooperation that the OIC views its indispensable role in shaping a culture of peace in a Multilateral World. The OIC has continued to expand and maintain its relations of cooperation with several international and regional organizations. These include, among others, the United Nations and its specialized agencies; Arab League; Council of Europe, ECO; EU; GCC; IOM; La Francophonie; NAM; AU, OSCE and the Commonwealth. In most cases, these relations have been institutionalized through cooperation agreements and memoranda of understanding, which entitles the OIC to reciprocally enjoy observer status.

The OIC was established and its Charter was based on the noble principles of peace, harmony, tolerance, brotherhood and equality of all human beings, as preached by Islam. The preamble of the OIC Charter reaffirms the commitment of its members to the UN Charter. It has, therefore, ever since its establishment in 1969 set for itself as one of its primary tasks, the realization of the principles and purposes of the United Nations. It has striven to play a positive role in the maintenance of international peace and security. The perceptions of the OIC member states, all of whom are also members of the United Nations, are identical to those of the vast majority of the UN membership on all important international issues.

The OIC has continued to support and appreciate the UN's efforts to combat the scourge of international terrorism and transnational organized crime, to enhance international security by strengthening non-proliferation regimes, the pursuit of universal nuclear disarmament and arms control goals, the promotion and protection of human rights, the attainment of genuine socio-economic development, its persistent and commendable efforts to achieve durable solutions to the problems of refugees. The OIC along with and its specialized organ, ISESCO, has continued its efforts to effectively pursue the extremely important and relevant theme of dialogue among civilizations. During May 2005, the OIC Secretary General held fruitful discussions in Madrid with the Spanish Foreign Minister on OIC's active involvement in Spain's initiative of "Alliance of Civilizations". Similarly, the OIC has also continued to support and appreciate the UN's principled positions and efforts to peacefully resolve the situation in the Middle East, particularly the Palestinian territories, the situation in Iraq, Afghanistan, Cyprus, Somalia, Sudan, Sierra Leone, Bosnia-Herzegovina, the ongoing peace process between India and Pakistan, including the Jammu and Kashmir issue, as well as the conflict between Azerbaijan and Armenia over Nogorni-Karabakh. Likewise, the OIC has shared with the United Nations its ongoing efforts to peacefully resolve the situation in Chechnya and the Southern Philippines.

Ever since its establishment and the deposition of its Charter with the UN in 1972 and the grant of Observer status in 1975, the OIC has continued to strengthen its cooperation with the United Nations and its specialized agencies. The two OIC Permanent Observer Missions in New York and Geneva, along with the Annual Coordination Meeting (ACM) of the OIC Foreign Ministers, held on the sidelines of the UN General Assembly sessions, have significantly contributed towards coordinating the position of member states on various international and regional issues as well as in regularly updating the OIC General Secretariat on UN activities.

As a manifestation of its cooperation with the United Nations, the UN General Assembly has regularly been adopting a consensus resolution entitled "Cooperation between the UN and the OIC". The latest resolution on this subject (A/RES/59/8) was adopted on December 6, 2004.

In recognition of its international stature, the OIC is one of the five organizations that have been invited to participate in the High-Level Plenary Meeting of the 60th UNGA session in New York on 14–16 September 2005. The OIC Secretary General has utilized this occasion to effectively project the commendable efforts undertaken by the OIC member states and the various OIC institutions in achieving the Millennium Development Goals.

As per practice, a high-level UN delegation participated in the 31st ICFM. Similarly, the OIC has been actively participating in all the High-Level Meetings between the UN and Regional Organizations. The OIC Secretary General has participated in the Sixth High-Level Meeting, which was scheduled at UN Headquarters in New York on 25–26 July 2005.

In addition, the OIC has also been actively participating in the biennial General Meetings between the Secretariats of the UN system and the OIC and its specialized institutions. During the last OIC-UN General Meeting held in Vienna from 13–15 July 2004, numerous proposals to enhance liaison and exchange of expertise in the political field, along with a series of joint projects in the areas of science and technology, trade, food security, agriculture, human resources development, environment, arts, promotion of heritage and education, were agreed upon.

Ever since his assumption of office, H. E. Professor Ekmeleddin Ihsanoglu, the OIC Secretary General, has persistently endeavored to promote global cooperation and understanding not only amongst the 57 OIC member states but also with the international community. In this regard, he has continued to undertake highly successful official visits to OIC states and interact with leading international personalities as well as regional and international organizations.

The OIC Secretary General's comprehensive statement during the 61st Session of the UN Commission on Human Rights in March 2005 received widespread appreciation and international attention and was referred to in the subsequent interventions by many delegations. The statement, interalia, focused on the socio-economic impediments in achieving the Millennium Development Goals, the need to effectively counter the alarming phenomena of Islamophobia and hatred against Muslims in the West as well as the plight of Muslim minorities in non-OIC Member States.

To conclude, there is a strong and urgent need in the 21st century, more than ever before, to reinvigorate the time-tested doctrine of multilateralism to promote international peace and security, with important international and regional organizations, including the OIC, playing their due role. It is indeed only through cooperation on an equal, equitable and just basis, rather than confrontation and the use of or threat of use of force, that the objective of establishing a culture of genuine peace and security as well as social and economic development, can be achieved.

ORGANIZATION OF THE
PETROLEUM EXPORTING COUNTRIES

ORGANIZATION OF THE PETROLEUM EXPORTING COUNTRIES

Establishment

The Organization of the Petroleum Exporting Countries – OPEC – was formed at a meeting held on September 4, 1960 in Baghdad, Irak, by five Founder Members: Iran, Irak, Kuwait, Saudi Arabia and Venezuela.

OPEC is a permanent intergovernmental organization, currently made up of eleven oil producing and exporting countries, spread across three continents; America, Asia and Africa.

The OPEC Member States are Algeria, Indonesia, Iran, Iraq, Kuwait, Libya, Nigeria, Qatar, Saudi Arabia, United Arab Emirates and Venezuela.

These countries have a total population of about 525 million and for nearly all of them, oil is the main marketable commodity and foreign exchange earner. Thus, for these countries, oil is the vital key to development – economic, social and political. Their oil revenues are used not only to expand their economic and industrial base, but also to provide their people with jobs, education, health care and a decent standard of living.

OPEC is headquartered in Vienna, Austria.

Executive Head

H. E. Sheikh Ahmed Fahad Al-Ahmad Al-Sabah, Secretary-General of OPEC

Objectives

OPEC's principal objectives are:

– To co-ordinate and unify the petroleum policies of the Member Countries and to determine the best means for safeguarding their individual and collective interests;

– To see ways and means of ensuring the stabilization of prices in international oil markets, with a view to eliminating harmful and unnecessary fluctuations; and

– To provide an efficient economic and regular supply of petroleum to consuming nations and a fair return on capital to those investing in the petroleum industry.

Contact Information

Organization of the Petroleum Exporting Countries

Obere Donaustrasse 93
1020 Vienna
Austria

Telephone: + 43 1 21112-279
Fax:　　　 + 43 1 2149827

Internet:　　**http://www.opec.org**

Organization of the Petroleum Exporting Countries

H. E. Dr. Alvaro Silva-Calderón, Former Secretary-General of OPEC

According to a United Nations Report on Human Security, between 1945 and 2000, an estimated 190 million people were killed directly or indirectly as a result of the 25 largest conflicts in the 20th century. In 2003 alone, we have witnessed the US invasion in Iraq, a more than seven year rebel insurgency in Liberia, civil war in the Ivory Coast, and so the list goes on. In today's multicultural society with people coming from all kinds of different cultural and religious backgrounds, we find ourselves in a place where we have become intolerant. The open door policies have vanished and we have no longer a need to invite the other in. Instead we are desperately holding on to what we believe to be rightly ours and fight in the name of religion, politics, ethnicity or racial superiority. Differences based on socio-economics, religious beliefs and cultural identification have driven wedges between us and the other, legitimizing our intolerance. Let us step up to the plate and face the dire reality that our actions are no longer sustainable.

As the famous saying goes "what comes around, goes around", which means the North's pollution becomes the South's droughts; conflicts in far off places, turn into a refugee crisis at our very doorstep. The South's deforestation becomes Europe's heat waves. Under the pseudonym called development we have carefully crafted a model that has proven to be flawed. Enhancing the lives of the haves, forgetting the lives of the have-nots, and in the process we destroy the very Earth we are standing on today. So whether we want to face up to the truth or not, humankind is interdependent and interconnected, but we are blind to its signs.

Let us listen carefully to the moans of mother Earth and try to interpret those signs. We have been given this planet free of charge, a life long rent-free lease, and this is how we have shown our gratitude. But there is something called payday, and we are now faced with a staggering bill. Natural catastrophe has taken a firm hold all around the world.

So how can we create a peaceful society? If we wish to achieve this goal, we need to realize that we are interdependent and interconnected, and thus must take the responsibility to partake in achieving sustainability.

Therefore, it is imperative to link peace with sustainable development, poverty, the environment, and the use of our natural resources.

OPEC is aware that its role on the world stage is pivotal in more than one way. For one, the role that oil plays in preserving peace by means of continuing to provide a constant supply of oil and gas, at a reasonable price level for both producers and consumers, rich and poor alike.

On the other hand, OPEC's overall commitment and priority is to eradicate poverty to achieve sustainable development in general and sustainable livelihood in particular. Economic advancement for developing markets, for the have-nots, for those lacking basic access to food, water, sanitation, health care facilities, and education, for those lacking the basic minimum requirements for human dignity, is a must. Therefore, the important role oil can play in the long-term equals poverty alleviation, which constitute ultimately one of the cornerstones of peace.

OPEC has worked hard to provide security and balance, as we have witnessed during the invasion in Iraq, where OPEC ensured a steady supply of oil at a reasonable price, despite market turmoil and oil production losses due to political instability in its own Member Countries Nigeria and Venezuela. The role of energy, in terms of boosting sustainable energy resources in developing countries, to expand economic growth and enhance the standard of living is in all encompassing in terms of achieving economic and commercial sustainability, as well as addressing environmental and social concerns. OPEC is an organization, which aims to make a multilateral contribution in economic terms, in terms of globalization and sustainable development. We must open up world trade, and that must include the developed world opening up its markets to the products of the developing world. It means another way in which OPEC could make a valuable contribution in terms of sustainable energy, and thus sustainability.

When we speak about North-South relations, we speak about the discrepancy between the haves and the have-nots. Essentially, we speak about an obligation to contribute to the South, where currently some 1.2 billion people live in extreme poverty, over two billion people lack access to adequate sanitation; over one billion people lack access to safe drinking water; and more than 8 % of children in lesser developed nations (LDC's) die before reaching the age of five. Furthermore, two billion people lack basic access to electricity. Developing countries are currently faced with the challenges of meeting the rising demand for energy service in an economically viable, environmentally sound, and socially acceptable way. An affordable effective and reliable supply of energy is therefore, essential to furthering sustainable development.

We can also speak about South-South relations, in which OPEC Member Countries aim to promote co-operation between other developing countries as an expression of South-South solidarity, and thus aid in sustainable development. By reducing poverty across the world, we would also indirectly help to resolve cross-border and domestic conflicts, reduce environmental degradation, as fewer people are forced to decimate their land to survive.

The OPEC Fund for International Development – a multilateral development finance institution – was established in January 1976, by the Member Countries of OPEC with the objective to combat global poverty. The Fund's resources consist of voluntary contributions made by the OPEC Member Countries, and lend financial assistance in the form of loans for development projects and programs, and for balance of payments support. The Fund provides grants in support of technical assistance, food aid, research and humanitarian emergency relief. They contribute to the resources of other development institutions whose work benefits developing countries.

The mission of the OPEC Fund is to promote solidarity among countries of the South, encourage co-operation between OPEC Member Countries and other developing nations and make efforts to contribute to the development efforts that these countries are already making.

The Fund's main focus is the poorest and neediest segments within these countries. With the backing of the OPEC Member Countries, the Fund has been allowed to expand and to broaden the scope of its activities. Therefore, there has been a slight shift in the mandate moving towards humanitarian programs, like those related to famine relief and the problem of HIV/AIDS. The problem of HIV/AIDS is for example one where, until recently, people did not realize how devastating it was for the world at large. More than that, HIV/AIDS is destroying the gains – both social and economic – that others and the Fund have made. In other words, these are small examples of how our world has become interdependent and interconnected. This is a case where we can no longer ignore our responsibility, because we are mutually dependent, and there is simply no way back. Thus, we can rise to the challenge called "Peace", by taking responsibility for each other, no matter what color or creed we are, as members of one family, for our children, and their children's future sake.

PACIFIC ISLANDS FORUM

PACIFIC ISLANDS FORUM

Establishment

The Pacific Islands Forum, formerly the South Pacific Forum, is the political grouping of independent and self-governing States of the Pacific.

The Forum was established in 1971 to provide Member States with the opportunity to express their joint political views and to cooperate in areas of political and economic concern.

The sixteen Forum Member Countries are Australia, Cook Islands, Federated States of Micronesia, Fiji, Kiribati, Nauru, New Zealand, Niue, Palau, Papua New Guinea, Republic of the Marshall Islands, Samoa, Solomon Islands, Tonga, Tuvalu and Vanuatu.

New Caledonia was admitted to the Forum as an Observer.

The Pacific Islands Forum has dialogue partnerships with Canada, China, European Union, France, Japan, Republic of Korea, Malaysia, Philippines, United Kingdom and United States.

The Pacific Islands Forum is headquartered in Suva, Fiji.

Executive Head

H. E. Mr. Greg Urwin, Secretary-General of the Pacific Islands Forum

Objectives

The mission of the Pacific Islands Forum Secretariat is to work in support of Forum Member governments to enhance the economic and social well-being of the people of the South Pacific by fostering cooperation between governments and between international agencies, and by representing the interests of Forum Member Countries.

In the area of regional security, the adoption of the Biketawa Declaration by the 2000 Pacific Islands Forum represented a landmark decision for the region. The region now has in place a set of principles which Members have committed their Governments to as well as a guide to regional action in the event of a crisis in Member Countries.

This has added a new dimension to the Forum's work on security issues and the Secretariat has developed an implementation strategy for the Declaration working in close collaboration with the Commonwealth Secretariat and the United Nations.

Peacebuilding programmes and Preventive Diplomacy/Conciliation Projects have been incorporated into the Forum Secretariat's working agenda.

Contact Information

Pacific Islands Forum Secretariat

Private Mail Bag
Suva
Fiji

Telephone: + 679 312 600
Fax: + 679 301 102

Internet: **http://www.forumsec.org.fj**

Regionalism and Peace

H. E. Mr. Greg Urwin, Secretary-General of the Pacific Islands Forum and Janine Constantine

"Leaders believe the Pacific region can, should and will be a region of peace, harmony, security and economic prosperity, so that all of its people can lead free and worthwhile lives. We treasure the diversity of the Pacific and seek a future in which its cultures, traditions and religious beliefs are valued, honoured and developed. We seek a Pacific region that is respected for the quality of its governance, the sustainable management of its resources, the full observance of democratic values and for its defence and promotion of human rights. We seek partnerships with our neighbours and beyond to develop our knowledge, to improve our communications and to ensure a sustainable economic existence for all."

Pacific Islands Forum Leaders Auckland Declaration, April 2004

In 2003, Pacific Islands Forum Leaders took the decision to review the Forum. They established an Eminent Persons Group of former leaders and diplomats who traveled the Pacific with a mission to find out, through extensive consultation, the sort of Pacific people wanted to live in. Their observations were embodied in an extensive report and in a new Pacific Vision which was adopted at a special meeting in Auckland, New Zealand in early 2004.

The Vision for the Pacific is for a region where peace, harmony, security and economic prosperity can, should and will be a reality: peace being, not only the absence of conflict, but also the pursuit of economic and social prosperity, something to be actively and creatively pursued.

To give effect to that Vision, the Leaders mandated the preparation of what has become known as the Pacific Plan for closer regional cooperation and deeper regional integration. The broad aim of this exercise is to identify and act upon those matters, which, in current circumstances, might benefit from a regional, rather than national approach. At the Leaders' request, the Plan has security, broadly defined, as one of its highest priorities, and the security related activities identified in the Plan have as their broad objective the building of peace and the prevention of conflict. Proposals relating to the Plan will be put to Leaders at their annual meeting towards the end of

2005 in PNG. If adopted by them, the Plan will, among a range of other issues, guide regional efforts in the areas of peace-building and conflict management.

In terms of process, a Task Force of Senior Officials and regional agencies has been charged with responsibility for developing the Pacific Plan. Initially, they are looking at sector by sector cooperation; identifying early gains, both for their own sake, and as a means of maintaining momentum; and also working on more general proposals for the future. The Task Force will produce a substantial but by no means final outcome for the Leaders which proposes practical advances and gives them a basis for judgement about how they might want to further the process.

Most importantly, the call for the Plan has, as an underlying principle, a strong recognition of the inter-connectedness of the issues the region faces. The Plan proposal was accompanied by other measures aimed at making the Secretariat, and the Secretary General more proactive. The development of the Plan will be a cumulative, open-ended process. It will be the work of years but will offer practical, cooperative gains in the shorter term. Among many other things, it has within it the means by which the region may address its security-related challenges in a much more comprehensive way. And that, in turn, may provide the best opportunity yet to meet potential conflict situations, if not at source, at least at an earlier stage.

This will build on the work of the Forum Regional Security Committee (FRSC) as the main regional consultative forum which identifies threats to security (broadly defined) and agrees on strategies for addressing them. Initially, the focus of this Committee was mainly on law enforcement issues but since 1997, after passage of the Aitutaki Declaration, the Committee has considered broader security issues. This Committee has become one of the most important Forum committees.

Quite what judgements one might make regarding the Pacific region's security condition are necessarily complex. There is a superficial view that the contemporary region is characterised by failure and chronic instability. It has become a common view in the halls of punditry that the region is an "arc of instability" with failed states, weak governance, endemic corruption and a uniformly negative outlook. That the region faces a range of challenges of these and other kinds it would be feckless to deny, and they require urgent, concerted attention. Additionally, it must be accepted that a number of Pacific countries face very particular difficulties relating to size, remoteness and resource limitations and that, relative to the international environment, these are likely to remain. While these difficulties do sometimes make it difficult to discern the future, it is important to remain clear about the stage the region has reached historically. Some appreciation of this does allow a degree of nuancing about the current condition of the region. Most of the countries in the region have been politically independent for 25–35 years. As a broad generalization, they have spent most of that time making good on expressing that political independence and they have done so, by and large, by employing the institutions and practices inherited at independence from the former colonial power. As time has gone on, some of those institutions and practices are being found to be no longer as useful as they once were. Throughout the region, people are thinking, casting around, and looking for ways to manage their affairs into the long-term future, quite acutely aware of the limitations circumstances have placed upon them, but fully aware of the need to find some practical answers. It is not at all surprising that such a process might be complex, protracted and filled with uncertainty. It is a process that self-evidently brings its own difficulties. It is not necessarily negative unless it exceeds certain bounds, unless it spills into conflict. If political will remains and if there are some sensible responses from external partners it also gives rise to quite a lot of genuine, if necessarily guarded optimism.

Overall, and despite the quite enormous challenges faced by the region, relative to circumstances elsewhere, the factors operating for the kind of dynamic stability the region requires remain quite considerable.

The Pacific is not a region crushed by oppressive regimes. It is not, in modern times certainly, a region bloodied by violent wars over generations, and it has, in a range of contexts, been successful in minimising conflict. It is, historically, a region steeped in strong systems of traditional governance and social discipline. It is a region with a considerable record of tolerance and solicitude. Where conflicts do occur, they barely register on those international databases that require a "deaths in conflict" rate of 25 per annum. A thankfully low death rate does not, of course, do anything to reduce the suffering and loss experienced by those in Bougainville, Solomon Islands and elsewhere through death, injury, dislocation, abuse and psychological violence.

The fact is that when conflict does occur in the Pacific, it often does so for some of the same reasons as elsewhere – disputes over land management and the utilisation of resources, the distribution of power, disparities between rich and poor. The sheer diversity of the Pacific – a strength in so many ways – can also complicate. And the

Pacific shares a range of the problems habitually associated with development constraints: low growth rates, pressures on natural resources, youthful populations, limited employment opportunities, urban migration, and systems of governance struggling to adapt. In short, there is nothing inherent about the Pacific, apart from its name, that allows the countries in it to rest more easily than others.

Notwithstanding that, it is a matter of fact that Leaders in the region have long recognised the need to address conflict related issues, even if the means by which they might do so have only developed over time. From the very early days of the Forum, Leaders brought peace and conflict issues to the regional table – the conflicts in South East Asia; nuclear testing in the region, the domestic conflicts in Vanuatu in 1980, New Caledonia, Fiji in 1987, and Bougainville, Fiji and Solomon Islands more recently. Since the early 1990s, the Forum has also been developing more formally expressed arrangements through which they might play a role in conflict situations.

The responses Leaders have made to regional conflict situations over the years have been cumulative, and it is partly this which has allowed our present Leaders to respond to the historical circumstances in which they now find themselves. They have done this in a range of ways, but, reference will be made to just two of them.

The year 2000 was, in a number of definite respects, the region's "annus horribilis". People, by now, found themselves grappling increasingly with a range of economic and social problems and thinking about how to manage their affairs for the long-term. Then, in the middle of that year, two dramatic sets of events took place – in May, the Government of Fiji and a number of other citizens were taken hostage in Suva's Parliament House, and shortly afterwards, in what some were tempted to see as a copy-cat event, the Government of Solomon Islands, against the background of some years of communal strife, was overthrown. Again, the Leaders sought to respond. The regional Foreign Ministers met in Apia in August 2000 to consider the situation, the first time this particular mechanism had been employed. They did not, on that occasion, propose immediate Forum action as the Commonwealth and the ACP group, both involving a number of regional members, were already involved with both Fiji and Solomon Islands at this point.

However, Leaders recommended that existing regional arrangements be augmented to allow the Forum to respond to members' requests for help in times of crisis.

So, when they came together later in the year in Kiribati, and in rather the same way as in Honiara eight years before, they adopted an instrument which they called the Biketawa Declaration which enunciated a number of guiding principles and possible courses of action considered relevant to circumstances of regional upheaval. Leaders "while respecting the principle of non-interference in the domestic affairs of another member state", recognised "the need in time of crisis or in response to members' request for assistance, for action to be taken on the basis of all members of the Forum being part of the Pacific Islands extended family". The Forum must, they said, constructively address difficult and sensitive issues including underlying causes of tensions and conflict. They went on to enjoin the Secretary General, in such situations to urgently initiate a process, as follows: The Secretary General was first instructed to assess the situation, make a judgment as to the significance of the developments and consult the Forum Chair and such other Forum Leaders as may be feasible to secure approval to initiate further action; consult the national authorities concerned regarding assistance available from the Forum; and advise and consult with the Forum Foreign Ministers, and based on these consultations, undertake one or a combination of the following actions to assist in the resolution of the crisis.

This involved: (a) a statement representing the view of members on the situation; (b) creation of a Ministerial Action Group; (c) a fact finding or similar mission; (d) convening an eminent persons group; (e) third party mediation; (f) support for appropriate institutions or mechanisms that would assist a resolution; (g) the convening of a special high level meeting of the Forum Security Committee or an ad hoc meeting of Forum Ministers; and (h) if after actions taken, the crisis persisted, convene a special meeting of Forum Leaders to consider other options including if necessary targeted measures.

This may appear a modest set of proposals, but they do have to be seen against their historical background. Biketawa is interesting, regionally speaking, in at least two ways. First, it amounted to the first explicit recognition that the internal affairs of a member state might in certain circumstances be the legitimate concern of the Forum as a whole; that the problems of one might be the problems of all. Secondly, it represented the first attempt, in a direct sense, to assemble a vehicle for conflict prevention, even though it was clear that the Secretary General, in particular, had to be very careful about arriving at the conclusion that a crisis situation might exist.

Biketawa has been invoked twice since 2000, most notably in respect of Solomon Islands. In 2001–2002, the Secretary General used it to explore possible avenues for the Forum and the Secretariat to play a role in bringing the conflict to an end.

A Forum mission to Solomon Islands in June 2002 examined the problems and, in July 2003, the Biketawa Declaration was the enabling mechanism through which the Regional Assistance Mission to Solomon Islands (RAMSI) was mounted. That Mission has been widely judged to have been a considerable success so far, although the restoration of Solomon Islands, even assuming relatively uninterrupted progress, will be the work of some years and the region will need to find ways of retaining the energy which will allow it to remain constructively involved.

The upheaval in Solomon Islands has demonstrated two related issues about dealing with conflict in the region. The first is that, once conflict erupts, the action taken to end it needs to be decisive; for too long in Solomon Islands the region prevaricated with well-intentioned half measures. Secondly, any such action needs to have as a pre-condition a sufficiently strong body of opinion in the country concerned that there is no sensible alternative to peace. Put simply, the Solomon Islands case conclusively demonstrates the extent to which for all its undoubted complexities, conflict prevention is infinitely preferable to conflict reduction.

The other occasion on which Biketawa has been invoked is in July 2005, by Nauru, in the context of its ongoing financial crisis. The Leaders, at their meeting in Apia in August agreed that the Forum should do all it could to assist Nauru. In the context of the developing process in the region, what the Leaders have directed represents the use of the Biketawa instrument at the conflict prevention stage. That Nauru is in a condition of crisis cannot be doubted, and the approach taken by the Leaders puts the region in a better position than it has been for a long time in respect of Solomon Islands, or further back, Bougainville. The adoption of the Biketawa Declaration was the point at which the Leaders acknowledged, in principle at least, that the problems of one might, in certain circumstances, be the problems of all. Against the background of recent Pacific history, that was a considerable step.

Biketawa and the broader aims of the Pacific Plan also demonstrate that the Leaders have accepted that the Forum must constructively address the difficult and sensitive issues which underly conflict. They know that conflicts repeat themselves primarily because the underlying causes of tension are not adequately addressed, that the means to sustainable resolution of a conflict depend on an analysis of their cause, and that the lesson to be learnt from repeated conflict is that if the real causes are left unattended, vulnerability remains.

Development of the Pacific Plan recognises that peace and security is closely linked to domestic failures of governance to meet people's aspirations for development and economic advancement. Threats to human security in the Pacific can foster an environment conducive to threats to geo-political security. While external criminal pressure involving international finance and smuggling of drugs, guns, goods, people and rare plant and bird species is serious and escalating, major threats to political stability in the region are more likely to emerge from internal dynamics which will contribute to threats from external sources. These include economic disparities; lack of good governance; social tension; land disputes; and other factors such as low levels of education, environmental threats, health challenges and food security.

One or two general issues are important in contemplating the nature of conflict in the region and its resolution to develop the interface between the formal mechanisms of government and society and the range of informal mechanisms potentially available. In part, this goes to the issue mentioned above about the stage in their history which Pacific countries are now reaching – the transformation, institutionally speaking, from a colonial inheritance which may have served to reinforce the top-down aspects of some Pacific societies, to a situation which might be more expressive of the totality of society's aspirations. Part of it too is about fashioning specifically Pacific modes of governance, and that means finding the right blend of modern and traditional practices. The validation of some of those traditional practices may well be the means of connecting government more closely to the people. However, partly because those very traditional methods may themselves not always be completely inclusive, more use needs to be made of the space which the full range of informal mechanisms allows.

A corollary of this seems to be that the first response to preventing conflict will often be at the local level. In Pacific societies, traditional or informal mechanisms of conflict management are often sufficient to dispel tensions. These mechanisms operating at a local level undoubtedly are not always fully representative of the populations of these communities – women and youth in particular can be absent from village meetings and from decision making that affects them directly. That said, Pacific island communities at all levels are making headway in the incorporation of all members of their communities in decision-making opportunities. In this context not only do women and youth need leadership support but so too do traditional leaders so that they can fulfill their role in peace building and conflict management in a world where many of the old certainties have gone. While many of these informal and/or traditional mechanisms have been the stalwart of peace maintenance in the Pacific over recent generations, their continued ability to maintain that role is being challenged by the range of 21st century realities. Finding ways to support informal and traditional mechanisms, making them both stronger and yet more accountable and inclusive, will need to be a central part of the region's agenda under the Pacific Plan.

In respect of those who may provide some of this support, that is, development partners, one of the lessons learnt from events in the region is that, in the search for sustainable peace, what is required is an ongoing process rather than simply an output (an agreement or accord). The process of developing and agreeing on peace is as important if not more than the final documentation which records that agreement – Bougainville and Solomon Islands are cases in point. It follows that ongoing assistance, once an agreement is reached, which is informed by this understanding, is crucial to giving long lasting peace a chance.

Many of the development assistance activities which take place in the region are clearly relevant to security related issues and peace building, in their narrower and broader senses. While the relevance might be clear enough, the explicit linkages may not, in every case, be so. It should, perhaps, be necessary to ensure that conflict impact assessments on all third party (i.e. donor funded) as well as Government initiated projects be a norm for development. Such assessments can analyse whether a proposed activity will exacerbate or create tensions, or assist in peace building by bringing together engaged groups in a constructive way. For example, the placement of water supply, a hospital or school can either act to increase competition for resources, or can bring communities together for a common good if the location, design, construction, etc. of that facility is done in a consultative, participatory manner. Similarly, supporting national infrastructure can be done in a collaborative way, genuinely transferring skills and building national capacity, or it can be done in a way which undermines domestic expertise.

Ongoing conflict prevention through development and social transformation requires a long-term commitment to doing all that is necessary to build and maintain a culture of peace. If there is one key message to regional and international players it is this – if you come to the region with assistance, you will be expected to come for the long haul and to come and work alongside those with national expertise.

The Pacific Islands Forum is attempting to reshape itself to better respond to threats to the security of the region and it is seeking to engage with a wide range of actors – civil society, including academics and peace practitioners; NGOs and grass roots agencies; religious bodies; and, of course, the protagonists in conflicts themselves; along with the Governments of the region. In order to improve this engagement with wide ranging stakeholders the Forum has asked that the University of the South Pacific (USP), the region's primary academic institution, help develop a Track II process, something which, in any concerted sense, has been wanting in the region and which will help channel the views of those outside Government into the Forum policy debate. Supporting USP is, in itself, a long term peace building initiative – the more the capacity of that organisation can be strengthened to help build the leaders of the Pacific's future, the more capable the region will become of creating the conditions to avert conflict in the future.

But there are also broader questions raised by the Leaders' Vision which those concerned for the future of the region need to contemplate. Just what is the Pacific region? Is it a genuine combination of like-minded states, held together by abidingly strong cultural affinities and shared experience in what is, globally speaking, a unique environment? Or is it, in essence, a historical construct, flung together by the whims of our colonisers, a region by default? What is to be the nature of the Pacific's relationships with the wider world? How are its small states going to find a place, one that pays some regard to their views and interests, in a globalised world? How will the region best interact with its neighbours, some of them very powerful and likely to become more so, on the rim of the Pacific? How does it most effectively interact with those parts of the region which have not achieved independence, the territories and other entities? And what is the future role, vis-à-vis the island states, of the larger, wealthier Forum members, New Zealand and Australia? To what extent – and allowing that their situations are far from identical – will they further develop their roles as full members of a Pacific Community?

All of these questions – and they are only some of those which are faced – are much easier to ask than to answer. The Pacific faces a time of rapid change and very serious challenges which need to be diagnosed and understood as accurately as possible in order to fashion adequate responses. To do that, the right questions need to be asked of the right people: the people of the region themselves.

While peace building is very much a matter of appropriate institution-building and policy making, it remains essentially one of values: the quest for peace is a quest for coherence or unity. In order for that quest to be meaningful in Pacific societies, those who assist in peace restoration must have a good understanding of what "coherence and unity" mean for Pacific people.

There is much to learn about how peace is maintained in the Pacific region. If we can learn to listen to Pacific communities, to hear the issues that cause disruption, and to see how those issues are resolved, we will be better informed on how to assist when required. If we can incorporate both external interventions with internal knowledge and skills we have a better chance to offering more relevant and effective assistance. If we can learn how to utilise mechanisms that already exist, at informal and formal levels of society, for peace and conflict management we will be better placed to assist the countries of our region to build sustainable peace.

ANNEX

About the Declaration for All Life on Earth

The Declaration for All Life on Earth, launched by the Goi Peace Foundation, promotes a shared vision of a truly peaceful and harmonious world for all life in the 21st century. It sets forth guiding principles to realize this vision and encourages all people to apply them in their individual lives and in their specialized fields of activities. Our collective wisdom and joint efforts are vital to ensure a bright and sustainable future. The Declaration for All Life on Earth is intended to serve as an instrument in bringing together individuals and organizations committed to this common aim.

DECLARATION FOR ALL LIFE ON EARTH

Preamble

The earth is an evolving living entity. Every form of life on earth is an important part of this living entity. Accordingly, we, as individual human beings, must cultivate the awareness that we are all members of a global community of life and that we share a common mission and responsibility for the future of our planet.

Every one of us has a role to play in the evolution of our planet, and to achieve world peace each of us must live up to our responsibilities and obligations. Up to the present time, few people on earth have been fully satisfied with life. We have faced conflicts all over the world in competition for limited resources and land. This has had a devastating effect on the global environment.

As we enter the new millennium, more than anything else, the realization of world peace depends on an awakening of consciousness on the part of each individual member of the human race. Today, it is imperative that every human being bears the responsibility of building peace and harmony in his or her heart. We all have this common mission that we must fulfill. World peace will be achieved when every member of humanity becomes aware of this common mission – when we all join together for our common purpose.

Until now, in terms of power, wealth, fame, knowledge, technology and education, humanity has been divided between individuals, nations and organizations that have possession and those that do not. There have also been distinctions between the givers and the receivers, the helpers and the helped.

We hereby declare our commitment to transcend all these dualities and distinctions with a totally new concept, which will serve as our foundation as we set out to build a peaceful world.

General Principles

In the new era, humanity shall advance toward a world of harmony, that is, a world in which every individual and every nation can freely express their individual qualities, while living in harmony with one another and with all life on earth. To realize this vision, we set forth the following guiding principles:

1. **Reverence for life**
    We shall create a world based on love and harmony in which all forms of life are respected.

2. **Respect for all differences**
    We shall create a world in which all different races, ethnic groups, religions, cultures, traditions and customs are respected. The world must be a place free from discrimination or confrontation, socially, physically and spiritually – a place where diversity is appreciated and enjoyed.

3. **Gratitude for and coexistence with all of nature**
    We shall create a world in which each person is aware that we are enabled to live through the blessings of nature, and lives in harmony with nature, showing gratitude for all animal, plant and other forms of life.

4. **Harmony between the spiritual and material**
    We shall create a world based on the harmonious balance of material and spiritual civilization. We must break away from our overemphasis on the material to allow a healthy spirituality to blossom among humanity. We must build a world where not only material abundance but also spiritual riches are valued.

Practice

We shall put these principles into practice guided by the following:

As individuals:

We must move beyond an era in which authority and responsibility rest in nation states, ethnic groups and religions to one in which the individual is paramount. We envision an "Age of the Individual" – not in the sense of egoism, but an age in which every individual is ready to accept responsibility and to carry out his or her mission as an independent member of the human race.

Each of us shall carry out our greatest mission to bring love, harmony and gratitude into our own heart, and in so doing, bring harmony to the world at large.

In our specialized fields:

We shall build a system of cooperation in which wisdom is gathered together to derive the most from technical knowledge, skills and ability in various fields, such as education, science, culture and the arts, as well as religion, philosophy, politics and economics.

As the young generation:

In the 20th century, parents, teachers and society were the educators of children, and the children were always in the position of being taught. In the 21st century, adults shall learn from the wonderful qualities of children, such as their purity, innocence, radiance, wisdom and intuition, to inspire and uplift one another. The young generation shall play a leading role in the creation of peace for a bright future.

May Peace Prevail on Earth

ABOUT THE GOI PEACE FOUNDATION

Masahisa Goi (1916–1980), a Japanese teacher, philosopher, poet and author, dedicated his life to peace and humanity. After witnessing the terrible destruction of the Second World War, he started a world peace movement to spread the message and prayer "May Peace Prevail on Earth" to unite the hearts of humanity transcending all boundaries of race, religion or politics.

To promote this universal peace movement internationally, the World Peace Prayer Society was incorporated in New York in 1988 as a non-profit organization. It was then recognized in 1990 as a Non-Governmental-Organization (NGO) associated with the Department of Public Information at the United Nations. The Society's activities are steadily expanding on a global scale with members and supporters worldwide working together to carry the message of peace to their communities.

The Goi Peace Foundation was established in Tokyo in 1999 with the approval of the Ministry of Education, Science, Sports and Culture of Japan, as a sister organization of the World Peace Prayer Society.

The mission of the Goi Peace Foundation is to bring together people in wisdom, united in their hearts toward the common goal of peace on Earth. By encouraging public awareness of peace and by building cooperation among individuals and organizations in all fields, including education, science, culture and the arts, we aim to build an international peace network to stimulate the global trend toward a culture of peace.

While cooperating closely with the World Peace Prayer Society through shared projects and networks, the Goi Peace Foundation pursues activities based on the concept and principles of the Declaration for All Life on Earth, the Foundation's vision statement for the 21st century.

The Goi Peace Foundation was granted Special Consultative Status with the Economic and Social Council of the United Nations in 2004.

GOI PEACE FOUNDATION CONTACT INFORMATION

The Goi Peace Foundation
Headquarters

Heiwa Daiichi Building
1–4–5 Hirakawacho
Chiyoda-ku, Tokyo 102-0093
Japan

Telephone: + 81 3 3265 2071
Fax: + 81 3 3239 0919

E-mail: info@goipeace.or.jp

Internet: **http://www.goipeace.or.jp**

For comments and recommendations, please kindly contact:
E-mail: goipeace@web.de